soft meteorites

Nathan Shepherdson

Nathan Shepherdson is the author of ten books of
poetry. He has been the recipient of a number of
awards including the Newcastle Poetry Prize, the
Thomas Shapcott Poetry Prize, the Josephine Ulrick
Poetry Prize, and the Mary Gilmore Award. He
is a sometime collaborator with artists and poets
including Pascalle Burton, Sandra Selig, Jonathan
McBurnie, Alun Leach-Jones, and Arryn Snowball.

By the same author

axolotl waltz
parallel equators
Pfft.. (with Jonathan McBurnie)
how to spear sleep
UN/SPOOL (with Pascalle Burton)
the day the artists stood still—volume one
clouds in another's blood
Apples with Human Skin
what marian drew never told me about light
Sweeping the Light Back Into the Mirror

Nathan Shepherdson

soft meteorites

UPSWELL

First published in Australia in 2024
by Upswell Publishing
Perth, Western Australia
upswellpublishing.com

Upswell operates in the city of Perth, on ancient country of the Whadjuk
people of the Noongar nation who remain the spiritual and cultural
custodians of this beautiful land. We acknowledge their continuing
connection to country and express gratitude to elders past and present for
their strength and creativity ... Always was, always will be, Aboriginal land.

ISBN: 978-0-645-87456-3

A catalogue record for this
book is available from the
National Library of Australia
NATIONAL LIBRARY OF AUSTRALIA

Cover design by Chil3, Fremantle
Typeset in Foundry Origin by Lasertype

for Eve

Contents

we were photographed

shovelling soft meteorites

onto our own graves

Luca Pescatore

1st house

(Bob,
Eugene,
Lucian,
Klaus,
Gordon,
Patrida,
Leighton,
Helen,
John,
Isma,)

an open door kneels sideways

i.m. Robert MacPherson (2021–1937)

you understood the successful energy in death,

knew how to replace shattered commas
with mended heads in any sentence
you were offered

you had a store of varying answers
toe tapping to the equation waltz
where (again) death is always the last one

standing

as its opposite gets to count itself

out

and you got to quip how 'Charon
stands on the bridge of a cruise liner
these days'

you received praise for your lists
of all things on which nothing
is written

a murmur beneath bark
plotting conceptual symphonies
no one else will hear

the hasty permanence
of unwatered trees fruiting unsilted ideas
in bent rooms

a cricket on concrete
ambling through coat hanger pelicans
on water only in the viewer's eye

rusted full stops
in colonial-blue bottles
next to your bed weigh more
than consciousness

your wit in its frog-skin pouch

your wide-eyed accent
dusted in the visual silence
of an even quieter man

the canvas the length of yourself
is the length you would go to
to see yourself

(out)

of the picture

() the brush
remembers the hand
when its artist
is gone ()

& decades after its demolition
you still sit down to ponder the daily special
at the Mayfair Bar

remake
the sandwich
into the subject
into abstraction
into itself

thought is butter.

camp beds
frozen in rumour
of their own absence

stencilled letters and numbers
keep army disposal blankets warm
as you direct yourself to stand

out

in the cold

to prevent others
from putting unnecessary things
on walls

this is / this is / this is
a fossil from a local freeway siding
in my fourteen-year-old hand
a gift traded with you
from its own time to then

you told me you took home the primed-white
from my father's four-inch house brush be/
fore he painted your portrait

both of you arrested inside your violently astute adage
about painting being plied then applied by 'a mammal
at either end' of the brush with yourself added on
you are a third mammal on Masonite®

the portrait a no-eyed seer
as you arrived denim-toughgh
your Sharpie phase self-contained
in the lidless triangles of your VW

the white-primer hopefully still starched
as the sheet on which your body was laid in stony colour
unable to see itself given the portrait is lost
until the portrait is found by the two-eyed needle
stalking its haystack → perhaps the same needle
that unpicked the time you went about
killing French art with a hammer

murder an end to get to where you begin.

always tell the joke to those who will never laugh.

in the Whitlam wonderland
hoovered up with bits of American dream
you left yourself alone (to sift through yourself alone)
to produce cashmere quality uncertainties
equal to your namesake's monogram goat

half/man
half/shirt

you left yourself
at the dry cleaners
to be picked up

later

(here) & (there)

two places
salvaged
to nourish
forgetting

(again)

evidence of the zero ←
used as a wedding ring
for life →

what you got away with →
is what you delivered
to us ←

windows are always asleep until you open them.

this one is closed.

upstares

for Eugene Carchesio

two speakers say nothing
when the work is
untitled

and money on the table won't burn
until they find a match (between)
the two thoughts on offer

a white cloth hastily draped
over the body of a pun
is (still) amusing

in the car on the way back
from the gallery you tune the radio
to yourself

and tell me, 'poets are born ghosts,
only become people
when they die'

LF/KK

imagining
the Lucian Freud portrait
of Klaus Kinski

a few extra pounds

hair the glare-grey
of morning fog

his skin
covered in arguments
instead of tattoos

his crazy stare
might escape the skull
with a knotted bed sheet

↓

powder-blue eyes
preserved as cufflinks
buttoned back through the lids
before burial

teacher

i.m. Gordon Craig (1928–2022)

if i plant the bible in the garden
all answers will grow
with equal satisfaction

the ears safer underground
where worms empty out from parade
on stave lines dissolving in drum rain

his hands follow keyboard lines
as easily as living scripture
along the mossy lip of a stone wall

the pocket watch in his chest
ticks kindness in counterpoint
to the heart

he knew many prayers by their first names.

the sun pulls him in the direction of its memory.

Xerxes tells us we should all sing to trees.

two by two

for Patrida Blake & Leighton Craig

with your ear
pressed to a bovine temple
you transcribe the message
from the hammer

enamel circles
that fall into
what they fell
out of →

(pupils) gamma-red
offer two corneas from one eclipse
before it inhales itself
as a squared shadow

(listing   )

a glass boat
yet to be built in a dream
yet to be slept is our ark
waiting for its enigmatic parade
of colour & consciousness
two by two

the flesh on this surface is memory
distinct from its inoculation of the senses
touch dispersed at this distance
is always recorded is always there
to harden bones in unknown meditations

in lush brush licks
a father is painted into the picture
and out of sight

in this small university
layered green with insights
we muster silence to intone its forms
but it can only point
to where we stand

even the thoughts of others
remain as self-portraits
of ourselves

two poems for Helen Franzmann

A.

what i imagine Eva Hesse
would have sounded like
at the keyboard . . .

strands of her hair
as stave lines

notes following sunlight
up the wall

painted hands laid out to dry
in the psychology & landscape

mangrove-mud sound
of unknown feet walking
through her body

hundreds of ping pong balls
wrapped in a soft parquetry
of eyelids spat from doleful rapids
coalesce in glare at the water's edge

the unquestionable peace
of infant breath

B.

we watch a crow stirring milk

beak in bowl
nothing other than clockwise
as an unpasteurised whirlpool
forms to imitate an arpeggio-powered
plughole always asking the same
question with its one eye open

unsurprisingly the tears of crows are black

the marbling no ice cream swirl
night pigments efficiently seduce
discontinued memories one at a time
like mountaineers loosening your teeth
before they fall silently
down your throat . . .

what says the feather
to the balding bird
on its short plastic perch
once a film canister brimming
with images of flight

one self for the other self
one self for now

whiting (36 × 36)

for John Honeywill

you convince the brush to replace the knife
to capture absent flesh with satisfied light from a fish
longer in name and body than the colour of its plate

in a slim Lent assemblage without the loaves our stomachs
blind to the art consumed as white-lipped shadows pray
in a secular way for their right to be seen

and you can see how a ghost in the tail
swam transparent as the V hooked from perseverance
open-mouthed onto its first and last taste of factory ice

this ophthalmic test levitates us to vertical behind
its crockery cornea cradling the head in its silver lining
with its oil-spill eye washing up on us as its memory

liturgy in llama land

i.m. Isma McGuckin (1934–2023)

asleep we recognise each other.

mackerel sky mixed in
with caramelised words
from the gospels according
to Frank Sinatra.

the day you met him
on the Gold Coast, his hair still
a comb-over from both hemispheres
balancing on his vocal cords
the hotel in which he stayed
and you never left.

even now
we can all sing
lyrics not yet written
into our memories
are remembered
nonetheless.

later, your honorary Doctorate in Generosity,
part of the boil-over from the magic Italian saucepan
where acres of sugar cane grew to match the hair
on your father's head for sweetness jammed between layers
of hard work as the packed lunch for unbending faith.

earlier, you became your sister
as an only child nestled between
your parents, who each plant their eyes
in your eyes, one on the new moon, one

on the full moon, above and below, into
soil syntax deep in farming folklore, where
you grew straight into the version of yourself,
as your parents continued to grow through you,
tendrils following you into a night-cave where clocks
become hearts once they die.

very much alive,
in your leopard-print-Lollobrigida-swimsuit,
the mirrors stop looking at each other, stop
looking at themselves, to look at you, in black and white,
70 years in a moment that confesses there is no point
in wounding the past.

today, you are the third funeral i've attended for your family.

in the same church, mid 60s modern, an A-frame with Tito toenails,
a timber-lined wedge in love with its maths, inverted, axe-edge afloat,
to split another atmospheric fencepost into open blue.

your husband, a 'Monk' of virtuosic taste,
who could train air to move around objects, who
collected tens of thousands of mouths, who used music
to fumigate life, until disease let quiet cyclones roll through his skull
with the cruel regularity of guard dogs with nothing to protect.

your son, the beautiful boy, complexion of fresh machine oil,
with a distant Eastwood squint, who perhaps recognised himself
too well at 61.

& your daughter, left to tidy each corner of this triangle, left
to work out how to wear the Lazarus-stone necklace, her being,
with the bone structure of a Christmas tree,
where the only decoration
is compassion.

( )

at that table, over there,
we all recognise the waiter,
because we can't see him.

at your table, we learned to eat time.

( )

and in continuing your dressmaker's art,
you demonstrate how to sew two bits of silk,
with a piece of tissue in between,

you pull out the paper
and you're gone.

2nd house

(Anne,)

framing references until the walls complain

for Anne Wallace

lost

lost to the ways of seeing
your eyes double in number
to consult the wisdom of the square
to serve appropriate evictions
to dig out and then replace
the nipples of Orpheus & Eurydice
with your retina to rib vision
as they stare chest to chest
before heading home

satisfactions

is it our satisfactions
that decide to attach commas
to our veins to encourage them
to leave our limbs with the millipede swagger
of an answer moving in all directions at once

your legs hanging out their Trewern window
with feet crossed in a caduceus pose
without the fangs

no movement in an hour and seven minutes

step

in sleep ←

your fingernails inflate
at the rate of one
per hour

& you get to watch a snowdome self
as the adolescent who is unaware that you're watching
yourself amble in jittery 8mm movements
through the ten stations of nostalgia

you resist the urge
to capture your own
attention →

to write the love letter
from your bare foot
to the glass

your right ear a convex landing pad
for clothed whispers to your Muybridge form

you both hesitate
before one of you
takes the eleventh

step

volumes

under a rolling pin
the lips of the couch
will speak volumes
on the relative comforts
of being able to die
with your boots on

when you spot the handle
it dissolves

always open the door
with your eyes
closed

(|)

this is is this
is this this is
a picture of the door
as it drinks from its own
shadow

or is this the door
itself

(−)

Greenslopes

when our grandmothers never met
at the Crown Stove & Foundry Co. cafeteria
they would each in turn recount then recant
the identical dream where ropes around their ankles
would pull them up with the force of a farmer's hand
in a hen house as a thirty-foot pole fell
to help itself to the skull of a man named John Heywood

later with curlew poise and caryatid complexions
the three women would face isolated corners of the room
where soft-ground etchings were lifted from their eyes
as buttons down their bloused backs leaked gaseous magenta

the fourth corner
was always reserved
for the dead man

♩

when we never met there either after school
after the factory had been abandoned
to its collapsible form with corrugated bruising
that exuded a drive-by-Böcklin-in-the-burbs dark
ratified as an iron smudge about to be crushed
by a giant industrial hand that still found the wherewithal
to bless our unpunctuated thoughts
with its leftover subtropical enamel

a boardroom for spiders
living well beyond
their tuxedo days

in our uniforms on a Friday
we stand on the embankment behind the factory
cut into the hill at Greenslopes

at our feet
dozens of over-wound clocks
lie on slat tongues in an orange crate

as is our ritual we hurl them one by one
at the wall or onto the roof simply because
Stephen Hawking no longer can

alarms breaking off-key make us laugh

tin percussion gut punching time with radium cloaked hands

exploded diagrams continue to scatter like thieves carrying Swiss
    jewel movements

walking home
you pause and sit to spread out the crêpe paper
you've bought to wrap your sister's birthday present
and we each drop a handful of wet full stops
simply to watch the colour run

our grandmothers are still alive

still flipping pikelets or pulling a date loaf out of the oven
still in their sunrooms where the outer leaves of African violets
are nurtured as chlorophyll catchments reading themselves as living
    parchment
as beckoned roots strike cilia-like in the potable aquatics of a jam jar

little survives
of the three-storey brick bell
at Sackville Street

Wednesday

every second Wednesday
an extra pair of hands
forms inside your body

they wipe down your ribs
to reapply the gold leaf
that projects soft-rippled striations
on the outer landscape of your lungs

they hang on for as long as they can
though once fully spent and emaciated
they slide out through the wound
tended to and kept open
by the gatekeeper of your anatomy*
named Thomas

(surname withheld)

*acronym GOYA

afterwards

afterwards

they pretend her ring finger
is a cigarette

knuckle sweet blood
an understudy ember
still aglow with cold pain

they think they can taste themselves
under the fingernail

afterwards

they drop her back
to her parents' house

the porch light comes on

the car drives off

dressed

dressed in every shadow is the light that edits it

ahum in the green weave in the subconscious canker
roots subdivide into their jurisdictions
deputised by the well taxed whim
from a nematode smile

uncalculated in any phrase
are words that acknowledge and suppress
this surface

happenstance freeze-dried
on a bank holiday of its own making
babysits the blood on the canvas sheet-singing
its sailcloth echoes amplified through the mouth
of a transcendental mask hung on the back
of a burning door (freestanding) on a salt plane
where an entire platoon of Lot's wives
look over their shoulders to watch themselves
disappear

(   )

behind the white rectangle
is a dictaphone that translates your breath
into the mineral bias of your colour chart

mercurochrome abstracts
reveal that even memories have knees
and although the roll call is unanswered by belief
the prayer is not far away

trivertebrae

i.   in vertical ground
a prototype for a mirror made of air is lost
along with the victim's handbag

ii.   at the arbitration hearing it was determined
that the skin exquisitely tailored to cover this light bulb
was mine

iii.   i trained three dogs
to dig graves
at your command

iv.   you find the magic spot along the hairline
that allows you to roll it aside
like a Lazarus stone

v.   you are shown the crop circles
left from dinner plates in new wheat
growing through the tablecloth

vi.   you talk about 'fidget lyrics' about lyrics that can bend a hyphen
      lyrics that move your Alsatian's water bowl across the verandah
      while you sip liquorice tea

vii. in a silent film where all the characters carry stop signs
      and constel the streets looking for the pot of red paint
      we'll never see

viii. semen smeared on the lip
      of a paper cup signals
      restraint

ix.   small mercies engulfed by large preoccupations
      still tend to your hair with the trickling caution
      of a blind gardener

x.   in vertical ground
      the upright burials
      of two failed organs

almost

almost as pre-purchased gifts from unwhittled discernment
your lungs relax as a pair of unused whistles
in a plush box

you realise you h
ave no enemies who h
ave not killed you
before

vigil

standing either side of the figure
we gently insert tallow wicks
in black crude in the well of each eye
for the lit vigil of memory-carved beings
who float as unframed prayers
as birdseed to the circle
through their regular overdose
on Euclid's 3rd law (where)
rhino whipped with their own radii
they see how they'll be staked
to opposite walls by their own end
points

the line having disappeared
never ends

sansevieria

trace elements
suffuse in a tarnished spoon
heated by a paint brush

in combustion

↕

repeatedly

you are asked to adjust the plimsoll line
that escaped its hull and now patrols the boundary
that demarcates the twin dwellings
where theory knocks on open doors
at unnumbered safehouses within colour & crime

now & again
you sweep up the flaked skin of philosophers
and tip it onto the sansevieria

its succulent biology urging donations
like fingers choosing to sprout
from a collection plate

it's been standing in its anodised jardinière
for as long as you've been standing
on the terrazzo version of your birth certificate

an object present
at the hourly reading of the will
left by the space it occupies

to prove that something is there
you must demonstrate that it isn't

the window is looking in

3rd house

(Sophia,)

lips over a waterfall

for Sophia Nugent-Siegal (1991–2014)

22.

following the taillights in a dream
along the mountain pass locally known as 'the ice box'
white lines doused in memory → absolved on undertaker tar → (ignite)

4.

the fog that walks into you never lifts
but lifts your body onto its untilled tongue
where your words are pollinated by hand

21.

& when her eyelashes were found as splinters in unknown hands
only the photographs were left to take the difficult questions
about when her body would be returned

1.

rinsing a cloud in grief
greyglo rheum yawns through cracks in a Shelley cup
cool lava seams exhaled through the calligrapher's hand

16.

the magnitude of →when← your lips were moved by someone other
    than yourself
the accidental unable to fall within its own definition
as witness statements are salvaged from those who were not there

19.

ears shout their mysteries at the same language
that turns stone to bread or preserves the skin from an apology
to transmit compound hope through the ribs of a dying star

7.

the talk was about attaining a certain state ←
how in slim moments a mirror could be gently torn into strips
which in turn reassemble themselves as each other

5.

they strip sleep from the windows
until they all break in complete harmony
with your last breath

18.

or → under a cloudless sky
how rain poured within the circumference of your umbrella
and how it fell clear but pooled red

6.

in the bottom drawer of all things
a folio of sketches packed in an ear-rustle of tissue
where exquisite lines record the salt forms in dried tears

10.

your soul smuggled out in a hollow stalk of fennel
3 hairs encased in the wax head of 1 ordained match
punished or unpunished ideas gauge regrowth in their livers

9.

evicted from your animal form →
the spine from your body and the spine from your shadow
hang like shoelaces over a gold doorknob

17.

heron-hymned feet firm on either side of the creek
her swaying body perhaps 30 metres tall
as she swallows oncoming arrows dipped in honey

8.

to flirt at this depth with an anchor
unsure if it can hold its own weight or iron mind
kelp-combed on the sea floor of an unintended world

14.

this is the current turning the pages of books in a shipwreck
a seahorse puppet-plays the movement in liquid maths
in sync with an undulating photo of a hummingbird in its pink hibiscus

11.

the 12 steps from this entrance to your image requires only 11 steps
    on the way down
slippage in the numbers that donate a percentage of yourself to the
    unregistered charity
in which your body as adhesive matter is injected into the time you
    were alive

20.

these calcium-set machines in which oil needs to weep to keep them
    moving
the theoretical pitch at which doors simply dissolve instead of open
the auto-luminescent quick escapes the nails to paint these lines from
    my hand to yours

13.

through a biscuit stack of lenses in a glasshouse Jupiter's Galilean
    moons become visible
4 dots that found their orbit after falling off the faces of dice in their
    universal crowd
400 years before ← named as Zeus' lovers 400 years after → your
    name affixed to earth

2.

blindfolded she stops on the spot where truth infiltrates the ground
small kikuyu continents edge along the fault lines of a question
where 22 crow feathers are inserted quill-first into transplanted green

15.

are there scriptures in the first rays of the sun
or is it simply a loyalty to death
that persists in auditioning time as our celestial accountant

3.

it's rare for any of us to meet the anointed shadow whose job it is to
    memorise our lives
to keep the appointment never made always broken yet never missed
to sit together to cut the apple to discover full stops instead of seeds

12.

this is the spur ←
that will emerge on the heel of a wooden crucifix
to prove your walk into eternity

4th house

(Gordon,
Samuel,
Arryn,
Stuart,
Pascalle,
Simone,
Ern,
Chris,
Ariel,
Noreen,
Luke,)

BIVT (10/40)

for Gordon Shepherdson

      e   e e

     e   e e
   e e
     e e
      e e
      e

e e   e e
   e   e e   e e e   e
e e

     e   e
       e   e   e   e
     e   e
e e e
e   e
 e

      e e
        e
    e

     e   e
    e e
   e e e   e e
 e

    e
     e
e e

o

o

o
o
o

o   o   o

o   o
o   o   o
o

o

o   o

o   o
o
o   o

o
o

78 soft meteorites

i

i

i

i   i

i   i
i i

i
i
i i

i

i

i   i
i
i
i
i

a

a   a

a

a   a

a

a

a a

a

a

a

u
u
u

u

u

u

u
u

an object may undo itself

for Arryn Snowball

de
scribe the light
to itself as itself
without look
ing.

to pin
ch the abstr
act between dis
located fing
ers.

how
to punish
the fleeting
with unsalted
perman
ence.

the
square ro
ot of indecisi
on is the squar
e root of ch
ance.

h
ow langu
age behave
s when it's no
t there when it's no
t langu
age.

64
corners sw
allow the invert
ed bodies of co-pi
lots without he
ads.

to e
ducate dist
ance to disap
pear without t
ravel.

burn
ing eyelids
as a source of fu
el.

you
can't see t
he black tong
ues bombin
g silenc
e with
full st
ops.

the sa
me meth
od is used w
hen performi
ng skin gra
fts on gra
vity.

an
other sp
ecies of windo
w to mock
the blin
d.

fla
tten the o
bject to infl
ate yours
elf.

anot
her flag to
mark this dea
th camp f
or theo
ry.

do
not tell t
he painter h
e's made a me
mo pad for g
od.

d
rain all surf
aces of all me
aning to prep
are all mean
ing for al
l surf
aces.

as
a way
as a way
as a way o
f falling into
our hands wit
hout time w
ithout fall
ing.

siding (plural)

for Stuart Barnes

he lives some
where south of h
is brain

sleeps war
m on an un
known h
and

is woken by t
he shadow of t
he same fight
er jet that w
ill never l
and

his e
yes dam bust
er bombs th
at smack t
he wall to re
lease the th
ief who will st
eal both of
us

in a me
asureme
(a)nt's lis
p our e
yes are e

ach two p
airs of sc
ales fro
m a py
thon's f
orgo
tt
en
eg
o

asifby

for Pascalle Burton

we wake up
& see our hands
have been seamlessly
attached to the other's
arms

<)our vision a soft mass
aggregate pupil happenstance
in unqueried left & right
combination(>

we agree
we can n
ever touch
again

penneggiole

for Simone Gelli

somewhere

between your mother's hands
& your father's mouth

you add;

olive oil
memory
& salt

to a plate of penneggiole mushrooms

(roasted)

where you were
is where they are

;

a tiny thatch
of pine needles
behind your ear

a sap circle
from a cut stalk
leaves an orange moon
on paper towel

reefwalkers

for Ern Grant

Dragon-scale

– whether in and about, she is likely to Pass
the northern sector; in the central sector; or towards
the southern sector; Certainly I have known people
who, in polite company, contained the world
by its initials, people who could "write" his initials
upon the surface of the coral.

when pronounced by the irreverent "harpoon" in this book,
whip-like, the vast majority eject themselves, go Beyond doubt,
to see primarily one thing; and one only; the living
acting as guides in unusual privilege; ......* –

Green carpet

And what did they want to see? – only ten months
before, they were destroyed by a storm of only moderate
intensity – a common ghost in shallow water putting
the visitor in touch on one hand, on the other; –
it buds off, carries a difficult dedication to The Still Authority
established to maintain a balance between Meg and I,
over the past forty years – and even in the garbage dumps,
in bright sunlight, moored inshore, – to go there to see that he,
or she: the living, mounted throughout the world
by Meg and her artist's-oil team tinting Up dawn:

Micro-atoll

treated to remove soft tissue, several workers have termed them
"planimals" in recognition of this, – , (it follows that living scientists
of repute will name the field down to their species level.)

crowned with a Pandanus palm, a square of about
forty feet tossed in my lap, I planned Quite suddenly,
then, we had to develop (or invent) a system of common
names for my collecting party, done to a high degree of
realism, the accompanying colour-plates, as specialist
stinging cells, have passed into routine usage,
derived solely from the study of the dead,

Purple Boulder

further identifications from the fact, from the Royal Commission
of the day, assume very different shapes and formations in response
to both the scope of the work and its visual impact.

wave-battered, or within a sheltered tide, is it
in deep or shallow water, or at a depth close to
direct competition, growing as its contribution
towards resemblance, in life, or in a library of
colour, offered to whatever word you choose –
a miniature islet surrounded by the complete;
I dumped the crestfallen diver overboard.

Cats-eye

on tiny stretchers that didn't roll and pitch,
I and my six police divers could rest at night,
when We'd come ashore towards dusk and
setttle down, talking shop – all of them within
the external colony, leathery, shipped back to the
mainland, down to six fathoms, damaging the third
day, I fitted a spare on the spot: to emphasise that
there were no more spares, discarded, I go through
the motions of taking back order, in a reef-rim,
in a dinghy too close to a skeleton.

Staghorn

: we'd return to the mothership and weigh
both engines in static, bringing us out of the same
spot, he yelled at me for nine days successively,
continued; until, on day twelve, still working, he
surfaces with glad tidings:

And I'd make reassuring noises, the effect that tomorrow would
be even better than today, more sceptical, frequently-seen,
in this little story, just in case you think the urgent removal
of a large group of animals arose in 1966, photography
had been sent to me, was offered only to the few;

Pink Finger

The individual, shed by the parent body is passed
along to the mouth, on an area of bare rock – aragonite
composed in nine-nine time – within a day or so, on either side
of the settlement, nearby the (Capricorn Group), cells in the
full-moon flatten, develop into a dome, as a small
cup-shaped structure, in a region of itself
that is, permanently November.

until a critical size is achieved; until another process
is found with a base that is wrist-thick or more; popular
misconceptions survive, neatly packaged as prey

Bookleaf

Once an assembly has built up into a tube-dwelling, a
tide-rim grotto, it survives indefinitely, And yet again,
– not so – When Meg and I guided VIP visitors,
it was essential to go out in advance to check
we were still living, to check that we continued
to grow at a normal rate, and that there still remains
the collective responsibility upon all of us to be the
subject, to find my companion, delicate, a reefwalker,
returned a month later in similar regeneration.

Unbelieving, I marked the spot –

Briar

pale blue material towards the centre is a feeding scar, part-exposed
by the falling tide, a half-ton of living disappearance better informed
than opinion will admit, on an overcast day, growth is stunted,
almost completely exposed, on the underside of dead
boulders, I have measured the peculiarities that
may be an appropriate place in well-being.

As these fall beneath, as superb rubble, they are taken into
the stomach as though they were theory, nutriment
for themselves – chemicals that are used among and
above a species of shelter, that grew itself in one year.

Needle

of course, I had to expand to grow horizontally
with the passage of years, back-bearings, in danger
of being overshadowed, the sharp vertical blades beneath
the brain can slash through footwear and clothing
at a touch, with ease, a perfect circular plate, rather
than an encrusting ribbon – many release sheets
of clear time, that appear to be drying-out, to document
immense debt broken down by thoughtless anchoring, to
document tropical deaths – so close to zero as made no
difference; this experimental area still marked on our path,

the physicist plays the piano

for Chris Gollagher

playing the piano
and talking in the same
                time (((((

the physicist says . . .

'we're all just one note
in this infinite sonata
and sometimes you get to play
the note and sometimes someone
else plays the note or sometimes
the note just plays itself'

that's it.

one note.

sometimes you hear it.

sometimes you don't.

sometimes it hears you.

sometimes it doesn't.

it doesn't matter
because matter is
its particle cavalry

it keeps advancing
even if you stop.

(a singing corpuscle
in the open palm
of pure gravity)

& even if there is an end
to this thing → this universe
→ it'll be propped up with
every idea there ever was →
or will be → thought or un
thought → and it'll be part
stave line part fence → and
there'll be all these notes →
stuck on it like horse
hair ←'

*

the physicist hits
the top note and
the bottom note
together

takes his feet off
the peddles

slams the lid

from a distance
he greets the door
as an old friend

and with each step

the door changes
from white to black
from black to white
from white to black

the physicist walks through
without opening it
without saying goodbye

*

(the next morning i see
the physicist's shadow
polishing the physicist's shoes
before retracing the physicist's
exact steps to the piano)

the shadow sits down . . .

((ages(((((

for Ariel Shepherdson

1.07   i watch her shovel time through a window

       pre-thrown dice build up in a midden
       pulsating with glow-worm gossip

       at the edge of all
       is the centre ←

       our skin cells undivided
       in dividing light

2.08   later, at the restaurant . . .

       the waitress approaches
       to take your order

       you look at her
       but say nothing

       she writes the word 'future'
       in pencil in her notepad

       then walks away →

letter torque

for Aaron Perkins

a.

as a new Aalphabet is released
like baby eels into a vortex
your vowels join hands

b.

is the skin of an alphabet
rewarded with truth
or meaning

c.

can death spell itself
in this alphabet where shunted horizons
hoard cold faces in each equation

hamartiologist board game

for Noreen Grahame

1.

```
OOOOOOOOOOOOOOOOOOOOOOOOOOOO
OOOOOOOOOOOOOOOOOOOOOOOOOOOO
OOOOOOOOOOOOOOOOOOOOOOOOOOOO
OOOOOOOOOOOOOOOOOOOOOOOOOOOO
OOOOOOOOOOOOOOOOOOOOOOOOOOOO
OOOO OO OOOOO OOOOOOOO OOO
 OO  OOOOO OOOOOOO OOOOOOO
OOOOOOOOOOOOOO OOOO OOOOOO
OOOO OOOOOOOO   OOOOOOOOOO
OOOOOOO  OOOOOOOOO OOOOOOO
OOOOOOO OOOO O OOOO   OOOOO
OOOO OO OOOOOOOOOOOOOOOOOO
 OO OOOO OOOOOOOOO OOOOOOO
OOOO OO OOOOOOOOOOOOOOOOOO
 OOOOOOOOOOOOOOOOO OOO OOO
OOOOOOO   OOOOOOOOO OOOOOOO
OOOOOOO OOOO O OOOO   OOOOO
 OOOOOOOOOOOOOOO OOOOOOOO
OOOO OO OOOOOOOOOO OOOOOO
 OOOOO O OOOO OOOOOOOO O O
OOOOOOOOOOOOO OOOOOOOOOOOO
OOOOOOOOOOOOOOOOOOOOOOOOOOOO
OOOOOOOOOOOOOOOOOOOOOOOOOOOO
OOOOOOOOOOOOOOOOOOOOOOOOOOOO
OOOOOOOOOOOOOOOOOOOOOOOOOOOO
OOOOOOOOOOOOOOOOOOOOOOOOOOOO
OOOOOOOOOOOOOOOOOOOOOOOOOOOO
```

2.

```
00000000000000000000000000000
00000000000000000000000000000
000000 0 0000 0000 0 00000
0000 00 00000000000 000000
0000 0 000000  0000   00000
00000000000000 0000 000000
 0000000 0000 0 000 000000
00000000 0 00 0000 0000000
0000000000000  00000000000
0000 000000000000 000 00 0
0000 000000000000000000000
 0000000000 0000000000 000
00000000000 00000000000000
00000000 00 0 00000   00000
0000 000000000000 000 00 0
0000 0000000000000000000000
0 0 0000000000 000000000 0
00000000000000 00000 000 0
0000 000 0000000  00 00000
0000 000000000000 00000000
00000000 000000000 0000000
0000 00 000000000 0 000000
0000 0000000000000000000000
00000000000000000000000000000
00000000000000000000000000000
00000000000000000000000000000
```

3.

OOOOOOOOOOOOOOOOOOOOOOOOOOOO
OOOOOOOOOOOOOOOOOOOOOOOOOOOO
OOOOOOOOOOOOOOOOOOOOOOOOOOOO
OOOOOOO OOOOOOOOO OO OOO
  OOO O OOOOOOOO   OOOOOO
OOOO OOOOOOOOOOOOOOOOOOOOOO
OOO   OOO OOOOOO OOOOOOOOOO
OOO OOOOOOOOOO OOOOOOOOOO
OOOOOOOO OOOO OOOOOOOOOOOO
OO O OOOOOOO OOOO OO OOO O
OOOOOOOOOOOOOOOO OOOOOOO
OOOOOOOOOOOOOO OOOOO OOO O
   O OOOOOOO OOOOOOOOOOOO
OOOO OOOOOOOOOOOOOOOOOOOOO
OOOO OO OOOOOOOOOO OOOOOO
OOOOOOOO OOO O OO OOOOOOO
OOOOOOOOOOOOOOOO OOOOOOO
OOOOOOOOOOOOOOOO OOOOOOO
OOOOOOOOOOOOO OOOO OOOOOO
O   O OOOOOOO O OOOOOOOOOO
OOOO OOOOOOOOOOOOOOOOOOOOO
OOOO OO OOOOOOOOOO OOOOOO
OOO OO OOOOOOO OOOOOOOOOO
OOOOOOOOOOOOOOOOOOOOOOOOOO
OOOOOOOOOOOOOOOOOOOOOOOOOO
OOOOOOOOOOOOOOOOOOOOOOOOOO

4.

OOOOOOOOOOOOOOOOOOOOOOOOOOOOOO
OOOOOOOOOOOOOOOOOOOOOOOOOOOOOO
OOOOOOOOOOOOOOOOOOOOOOOOOOOOOO
OOOOOOOOOOOOOOOOOOOOOOOOOOOOOO
OOOOOOOOOOOOOOOOOOOOOOOOOOOOOO
 OOO OO OOOOO OO O OOOOOO
 O OOOOO O OO OOOO OOOOOO
OO OOOOOOOOOOOOOOOOOOOOOOO
OOOOO OOOOOOO OO OOOOOOO
OOOO OO OOOOOOOOOO OOOOOO
OOOOOOOOOO OO OOO OOOOOO
OOOO OOO OOO OOOOOO OOOOOO
 OO O OOOO OOO OOOOOOO
OOOOOOO OOOOOOOOOO OO OOO
  OOOOOOOOO OOOOOOOOOOOOO
OOOOOO OOOOOO OO OOOO OOO
 OOO OO OOOOOOOOO   OOOOOO
OOOOOOOOOOOO OOOOOOOOOO
OO OOOO O OOO OO OOOOOO
OOOOOOOOOOOOOO OOOO OOOOOO
OOOOOOOOOOOOOOOOOOOOOOOOOOOOOO
OOOOOOOOOOOOOOOOOOOOOOOOOOOOOO
OOOOOOOOOOOOOOOOOOOOOOOOOOOOOO
OOOOOOOOOOOOOOOOOOOOOOOOOOOOOO
OOOOOOOOOOOOOOOOOOOOOOOOOOOOOO
OOOOOOOOOOOOOOOOOOOOOOOOOOOOOO

5.

```
OOOOOOOOOOOOOOOOOOOOOOOOOOOOOO
OOOOOOOOOOOOOOOOOOOOOOOOOOOOOO
OOOOOOOOOOOOOOOOOOOOOOOOOOOOOO
OOOOOOOOOOOOOOOOOOOOOOOOOOOOOO
OOOOOOOOOOOOOOOOOOOOOOOOOOOOOO
OOOOOOOOOOOOOOOOOOOOOOOOOOOOOO
OOOOOOOOOOOOOOOOOOOOOOOOOOOOOO
OOOO    O OOOO OOO   OOOOOOO
OOOOOOOO OOOO OOOOOOOOOOOO
OOOO OO OOOOOOOOOO OOOOOO
OOOOO OOOOOOO  OOOO OOOOOO
OOOOO OOOOOOO OO OOOOOOO
 OO OOOOO OOOOOOOO O OOOOO
OOOOOOOOOOOOOOOOO OOOOOOO
OOOO OO OOOOOOOOOO OOOOOO
OOOOO OO OOOOOOOO    OOOOOO
OOOO OOO OOO  OOOO  O OOOO
OOOO OOOOOOOO OOOOO OOOOOO
 OO OOOOO OO OOO OOOOOOOO
OOOOOOOOOOOOOOOOOOOOOOOOOOOOOO
OOOOOOOOOOOOOOOOOOOOOOOOOOOOOO
OOOOOOOOOOOOOOOOOOOOOOOOOOOOOO
OOOOOOOOOOOOOOOOOOOOOOOOOOOOOO
OOOOOOOOOOOOOOOOOOOOOOOOOOOOOO
OOOOOOOOOOOOOOOOOOOOOOOOOOOOOO
OOOOOOOOOOOOOOOOOOOOOOOOOOOOOO
```

6.

```
000000000000000000000000000
000000000000000000000000000
000000000000000000000000000
000000000000000000000000000
 00000000000000000000000000
0000  0 000000000  0000000
000   000 00 00000 000 00 0
0000 000000000000000000000
00000 00000000 00000000000
000   000 00 000000 00000 0
0000 0000000000000000000000
0000000000000  00000000000
0000 00 00000000000 000000
 0000000000 0 00000000 000
00000000000000 00000 000 0
00000000 00 000000000 000
00000000000 00000000000000
0000000000000  0000 000000
0 00 00 000000 00 0 000000
00000000000000 0000 000000
0000 00000000   0000000000
000000000000000000000000000
000000000000000000000000000
000000000000000000000000000
000000000000000000000000000
000000000000000000000000000
```

7.

OOOOOOOOOOOOOOOOOOOOOOOOOOOO
OOOOOOOOOOOOOOOOOOOOOOOOOOOO
OOOOOOOOOOOOOOOOOOOOOOOOOOOO
OOOOOOOOOOOOOO OO OO OOO O
OOOOOOOOOOOOO OOOOOOO OOO
OO O OOO OOOOOO O OOOOOOO
OOOO OOOOOOOOOOOOOOOOOOOO
OOOOO OOOOOOO OO OOOOOOO
OOOO OOOO OOOOOO OOOOOO O
OOOOO OOOOOOO OO OOOOOOO
 OOOOOOOOOO OOOOOOOOOOOOO
OOOOOOOOOO OOOOOOOOOOOOO
OOOO OO OOOOOOOOOO OOOOOO
 OOO OOOOOOOOOOO OOOOOOO
OOOOOOOOOOOOO OOOOO OOO O
OOOO OOOOOOOOOOO OOOO OOO
OOOO OOOOOOOOOOOOOOOOOOOO
OO   OOOOOOOO OO OOOOOOO
OOOOOOOOOOOOO OOOO OOOOOO
OO OOOOOOOOOOOOOO OOOOO
OOOOO OOOOOOO OOOOOOOOOO
OOOOO OOOOOOOOOOOOOOOOOO
OOOOOOOOOOOOOOOOOOOOOOOOOOOO
OOOOOOOOOOOOOOOOOOOOOOOOOOOO
OOOOOOOOOOOOOOOOOOOOOOOOOOOO
OOOOOOOOOOOOOOOOOOOOOOOOOOOO

indelible watermark for birth certificates

for Luke Shepherdson

'' '' '' '' ' '' ' '' ' '' '' ' ' '' ' '' ' '' ' '' ' '' '' ' '' '' '' '' '' '' '' '' ' ' ' ' '' '' '' ' '' ' ' '' ' '' ' '
' '' '' '' ' ' ' ' '' '' '' '' '' '' ' ' ' '' ' '' ' ' ' ' ' ' ' ' ' ' ' '' '' '' '' '' ' '' '' '' ' ' ' '' ' ' '' ' ' '' ''
' '' '' '' '' '' '' '' ' ' ' ' ' '' ' ' ' '' '' '' '' '' ' ' '' ' ' ' ' ' ' ' ' ' ' '' ' ' '' '' ' '' '' '' ' ' '' ' '
' ' '' '' '' '' '' '' ' ' ' '' '' '' '' ' ' '' ' '' '' '' ' ' ' ' '' ' certificates ' ' '' ' '' ' '' '' '' ' ' '' '' ' '
' '' '' '' '' '' '' '' ' '' ' '' ' '' '' ' ' ' '' '' '' ' ' ' ' ' ' '' ' '' '' ' ' ' '' '' ' ' ' ' '' '' '' ' '' ' ' '' ''
' '' '' '' '' '' '' ' ' ' ' ' ' ' ' '' '' ' '' '' '' '' ' ' '' '' ' '' '' '' ' ' ' ' ' ' ' '' ' '' '' ' ' ' '' '' ' '' ''
' '' ' ' ' ' ' ' ' '' '' '' ' '' ' '' '' '' '' '' '' '' ' ' ' ' ' ' ' '' ' ' ' '' ' ' '' ' ' ' ' '' '' ' ' '' '' ' '' ''
'' '' '' '' ' '' '' ' '' '' '' '' ' '' ' ' ' ' ' ' '' '' '' ' '' ' ' '' '' '' ' '' ' ' '' '' '' '' '' '' ' '' '' ' '' ''
' '' '' '' '' '' ' ' '' '' '' '' ' ' ' ' '' '' ' ' ' ' ' '' '' '' '' ' '' ' ' ' '' ' '' '' '' '' '' '' ' '' '' ' ' '' ''
'' '' '' '' '' '' ' '' '' '' ' ' ' ' ' '' ' '' '' '' ' ' '' ' ' ' ' ' ' '' '' '' ' ' ' '' ' ' '' ' '' '' '' ' ' '' '' ''
' '' '' '' '' ' ' ' ' ' ' ' ' '' ' '' ' '' '' ' ' ' '' '' '' '' ' ' '' '' ' '' '' ' '' ' ' '' '' ' '' '' ' ' ' '' ' '' ''
' ' ' ' ' '' '' '' ' ' ' '' ' '' '' ' '' '' ' '' '' ' ' ' '' ' ' ' ' '' '' '' ' ' ' ' '' '' '' '' '' '' ' ' '' ' ' ' '' ''
' ' ' ' ' '' '' ' ' ' ' ' ' '' '' '' ' '' '' '' ' '' '' '' ' ' ' ' ' ' '' '' '' '' ' ' ' '' ' ' '' '' ' '' '' '' ' '' ''
'' ' ' ' ' ' ' '' ' '' ' ' '' '' ' '' '' ' '' '' '' ' '' '' '' ' ' '' '' ' '' '' '' '' ' ' ' ' '' ' '' '' ' ' ' '' ' '' ''
' ' ' ' ' ' ' ' '' ' '' '' '' '' ' '' '' ' '' '' '' ' ' '' '' '' '' ' ' ' ' ' ' '' ' '' ' '' ' '' '' ' '' '' '' ' '' ''
' '' ' '' '' ' ' ' ' ' ' ' ' ' ' '' '' ' '' '' '' ' '' '' '' '' '' '' ' ' ' '' '' '' ' ' ' '' '' ' '' '' '' ' ' '' '' '
' '' ' '' '' '' '' '' ' '' '' '' '' ' ' '' '' '' '' ' ' ' ' ' ' ' ' ' ' '' '' '' ' ' ' ' '' ' ' '' ' '' ' '' '' ' ''
' ' ' ' ' ' ' '' '' '' ' ' ' ' ' ' ' '' ' ' '' '' '' '' '' '' ' ' ' '' ' ' ' ' ' ' ' ' '' '' ' '' '' ' ' '' ' ' '' '
' ' '' '' ' '' '' '' '' ' '' '' '' ' ' ' ' ' ' ' '' '' ' ' '' ' '' ' '' ' '' ' ' '' '' '' '' '' '' '' ' '' ' ' ' '' '' '
' '' '' '' '' '' '' '' ' ' ' '' '' '' '' ' ' '' ' '' '' ' ' ' ' '' ' '' ' '' '' ' ' ' '' '' '' ' '' ' '' '' ' ' ' '' ''
'' '' '' '' '' '' '' ' ' ' ' '' '' '' '' ' '' '' '' '' ' '' '' '' ' ' ' ' '' ' '' '' ' '' ' '' '' '' ' ' ' '' '' ' '
' '' '' '' '' '' '' '' '' '' ' ' '' ' '' '' '' ' '' '' '' '' '' ' ' ' ' ' ' ' '' '' '' ' '' ' '' '' ' '' ' ' '' ' '' ' '
'' ' '' '' ' '' '' '' '' ' '' '' ' '' '' ' '' '' '' '' '' '' '' ' ' ' '' '' ' '' '' '' '' '' '' '' ' ' ' '' '' ' '' ''
' ' ' ' '' '' '' '' '' '' ' '' '' '' '' ' '' '' '' '' ' ' ' ' '' '' '' '' '' '' ' '' '' '' '' '' ' '' ' '' '' '' ' ' ''

stars refuse to open their eyes until the planet is returned to its owners

5th house

(Davida,
Michael,
Maureen,
Kylie,
Lincoln,
Suzanne,
Eve,
Allana,
Maria,)

blue dust

for Davida Allen in memory of Michael Shera

edges do not forget
where they are or how close
you are to them

the horizon
a tugboat rope
around your ankles

as glass memory is poured from you
into the corner of a giant eye
buoyant in a still sea

tears from the fingertips
salt down organs inside words
used in a lifetime

a tongue transparent
against blue dust
in its brittle sky

note holding in the density chorus

for Maureen Hansen

all energy
in all objects
addresses its surface.

the mirror spawns.

corneas tossed in
with casino chips
of colour.

the eye the only ladle
with which you can sip
yourself →

even the colossal leaves fingerprints.

the onion converted to the thought
shoots itself and is eaten raw.

shadows are food.

this is the brush
that followed its own recipe
to its own death.

made mention of things not said.

dense patterns over white wounds.

can you ask for yourself back
once you've given yourself away.

or talk to a lost framer
who's never stretched anything
other than skin.

you set out
to name opposite corners
with the same time.

remember what they were
to forget what they'll be.

remember where you're going
to forget where you are.

subject to the rumour
is a pliable truth at hand
as you (again) teach yourself
to nail pictures to a wall
with a glass hammer.

a rope at either end of itself is still a rope
for Anna Jacobson

before i arrived, you'd already peeled the lines
off both hands, hanging them to dry like hand-rolled
spaghetti on dowel

now you demonstrate how to let your hands fall loose,
limber them in opposite circles, a pre-concert approach
to a glass keyboard, or a new mother testing warm water,
surface chime in a solid tub on a table, clean towels under
everything, including the rest of your life,

now it's the fingerprints that fall loose

within minutes they dangle at ground length, their first sway
in breeze, palpable relief, an impossible gift to their first sigh in
straightened circumstance, raw cotton spines unhemmed in Dervish
expectation, they walk air to its mint lung

you ask me to cut all ten rolags with dressmaker scissors that belonged
to your grandmother, steel-thigh sound the same as cutting Poland
from a canvas-backed map still flapping in an empty classroom

you begin the process of laying the rope from your own touch, tendrils
of liquorice-light entwined with bald fingers, you slip into the zone, a thin
halyard attached to a thinner heaven, it lets you up to pull it down, easy
and safe to float your body to the ceiling, suburban steps in the silent dance
without the need to move, all the while as the rope takes shape you repeat
your intrinsic mantra,

for the hand
to grip what is made
of the hand

for the hand
to grip what is made
of the hand

later, you tell me that MemorY gets tired of its 24-hour shift,
handwriting birth certificates for every moment, black paper
for night, white paper for day, trying to put fallen cliffs together
with only saliva and adhesive promises half-hidden in sequences
of doubt, the inkwell in each eye always running dry, too ready to
greet you with another hollow echo, and another half-price bouquet
of wilted transcription

you show me the finished product, the rope, how it floats when you
let it go, how it gets heavier when you mutter names from objects,
its colour an under-skin blue, prospected along a vein-range from an
aerial view of the back of your hand, turned over, reveals the gripless
milk complexion tight across your open palm, but of course you know,
and then i notice, as we both smile, because the rope has no shadow

you tell me it's ten times stronger than spiderweb, much easier to handle,
catches nothing by being open to everything, can muster savage clouds
in a boardroom, it lasts for months at a time, where, strung across your
rented lounge room, birds of all persuasions, from condor to canary, all
perch on it, watch over you as you sleep, weavers and winged masons,
beak-bundle your thoughts, to rebuild the necessary nests in your brain,
either camouflaged or highly coloured, the film in your memory is always
replaced before you wake,

morning feathers
on the carpet your pillow
for the next night

library for paper tongues

for Kylie Johnson

inside the vessel
is the vessel
you're in ←

the fingertips also syllables
as you peel echoes
from a clay cave

wet earth
shaped to a socket
for the viewer's eye

lips approach the rim of the object
like it's a circular tightrope where two words
press into one line

winter light frames its shadows
to build a bridge for your body
to reach sleep

hand painted birds
invent real feathers to sweep cold air
towards their D'Aguilar horizon

in every asking, one beat of a wing
does not ensure the answer
has somewhere to land

the one thing
you remember is everything
you forget

memory always the receipt
in the extra pocket
you don't have

at arm's length to the wheel
you spin yourself
into familiar absence

you watch a linen-look stowaway
supersede her glass turnstyle
to proffer kiln-fired freedoms

in the journal
of your dark-haired sister
you read yourself aloud

and should you ask yourself
if the smashed teeth of a nun
still glow like gingko gems

and did you overhear someone remark
'words tell the same story as arrows
without the blood'

finger to temple
the sun contemplates what to write
as its retirement age

corners drift to the circle
where silent mermaids wait
for the tide to return

→ the bell rings your hand.

→ lightning paints your toenails with a prayer.

standing

for Lincoln Austin

we were shown the bones
of a 20ft diamond

how something
could be born into →
yet orphaned from ←
its own light

a cage turned inside-out
like the shirt of a geometric god
offers its freedom for yours

even stones wilt at this angle

mirrors all teeth in your reflection

safety in the radiance of its core
that blinks the lost language
of a diving bell without water

we trust in what we see
only until it sees us

our personal horizons
neatly coiled in a drawer
before one swallows the key
belonging to the other

your smiling head
on its quantum
pillow

itself
asleep in fluid
dimensions

disruption centrefold

for Suzanne Archer

what perspires in the line
is the line that breathes
through the hand

as shadows vacate black for red
the third arm accretes rhythm
to form

the daily signature	not seen
on a daily contract	not seen
for light	( )

as narrow as the film
in a drowned camera stabilising
the headstone in each idea

→ sing the hurry
into the canvas cage
to release yourself

→ thump the energy
that makes the door
instead of opening it

()

a mirror is turned inside out like a sock.

a comma is suffocated with a leaf.

if you choose to disappear it'll be in blue.

()

the skin of the painting
redirects your finger
to its touch

the skin on the painting
is an anagram for continuation
and defeat

solid roads going nowhere
only decide to speak
when you arrive

trellises and arcs worry the limbs
into lit candles crawling
from the nearest cave

blood in its elastic nightgown
hangs us in cold sleep
hangs us to stop the needle
finding the thread
unquivered in saliva
graced on your mother's lip

or

is it the ceiling
that hangs from us
as we look down
on ourselves losing
count of unstained thoughts
climbing in and out in and out
from renovated suture lines
darkening like boiled ink

remnant of that little earth
quake called
birth

it's too easy for blood
to do its impression
of rain

the chapter on remorse
destined to be spelled out
with eyeballs in the sand

()

we're all a bag of calcium sculpture anyway.

elbows are good earplugs when you really listen.

dust only as loud as the feather that falls as loud as dust.

()

shred the everlasting into now   (   )
before it gets to realise the brand of time
it is → ←

chaos laced to a velvet tongue is still chaos.

and

if someone asks you
if you're the square root
of an angel

what would you say?

and

if someone questions
if you're the square root
of a ghost

would you just say yes?

()

here is the proof   (   )
you can talk about death
like the weather   (   )

()

your scream all the louder without sound.

Quintilis

for Eve Fraser

pulling words through faces
our eye colour dissolves into the molten audience
of a mirror waiting for its light to come home
unannounced like the tree that bought
its own leaves at auction

pulling faces through words
we unshun the distance in lips that mimic
the language in clouds remaindered on a shop floor
where one day is equal to all the moves
two chess players swap in a dark square

light never mended is never made

i.m. Allana Noyes (1964–2023)

was the photographer
in your life the only one
who knew you also had
a botanical name?

the shuffle of lips
in an unopened drawer
the easiest way to pull the string
in a stiff bundle of whispers
that turn puce as they flow
out of our ears → to try
to rehabilitate themselves
as memories that'll never quite fit
now that one of us
is gone

at 19 i had trouble
telling the difference
between your long hair
and a ladder

i'd lost a stone and a half
in 10 days when you appeared
with David with a cassette you'd recorded
your vocalese sweeping dry piano
into the corners of my room
which unlike me was still
able to stand

perhaps a year or two later
Gordon paints a red triangle
next to your ear ← a type
of snowplough for dark thoughts
rocked to sleep on the shoulders
of your black coat in oil

your sinus deeply planted in cigar smoke
tried its best to leave your body but instead
left your image behind

now is impossible to spell.

we shared a birthday
while our mothers
kept talking

the small shock
of the starter's gun
in the same year as it
coughed out its cartoon flag
as a swaddle cloth depicting a
smouldering question mark

the shadow curl
of apple peel hanging
from the sun

we followed words
up a twin set of stairs
in the same house but
on a divided range

now is impossible to spell.

as an actor
you convinced the words
you'd picked by an imaginary
roadside as you walked centre stage
to ask us with block-and-tackle look
in your eyes to come closer
to come closer to remodel
our lungs into spongey chairs
unticketed yet privileged
in this obedient game
devoted to opportune
listening,

now is impossible to spell.

(now)
is impossible
to spell.

& what did you do
when you found your body
on the page?

no doubt you just moved it
so you could keep learning
your lines

it's clocks as drink coasters isn't it?

your laugh
a kettle drum
of good will

your laugh
a cavern-carving row
of notes that the soft applause
on a white page has no chance
of carrying to your
requiem

in Hebrew your name
celebrates the birthday
of trees

trójkąt

for Maria Agoston

1.

with our nervous feet
comfortably fitted out in new words
we walk into the next conversation

2.

are there things
we can tell a language
that we cannot tell ourselves

3.

and if i told you where the full stop was
would you pick it up straight away
or wait until i'm gone

6th house

(Neil,
Rita,
Joe,
Gil,
Kathryn,
Ian,)

colour slides

i.m. Neil Portley (1933–2022)

1.

your mother & my mother
slowly parachute their shape
into your head

three foreheads aglow
carefully peeled like brushstrokes
from a full moon

three heads on three pillows
in stencil overlay in two generations
in one ancestral skull caught in its eclipse

2.

wherever the future was

you were

curiosity the ready currency
lining your pockets
on long walks
to the self

you bought into your own time

made mirrors from acrylic compounds

found it easy enough
to use a question mark
as a fork

3.

your ears
as gold cufflinks
in a box

so we can wear them
on white collars around our wrists
and listen to what your hands
were thinking as they held objects
up to analysis to decipher their design
as things with which you adapt
your own being

you worked on truth
with a soldering iron

4.

narrow stems
in your wife's garden
in Thurlby Street
lean then rotate
towards your memory

5.

as a young man
the motorbike didn't take the corner
but you did

jigsaw anatomy
in a skin box

polio flashbacks
in hospital fog

unapprehended shadows
lean over you

never introduce themselves

in all this distortion
you wonder how
you'll be carried
into the next century

to old age

*

earlier that week
as a young man
as a lab assistant
in his white coat
at the Physiology School
you stroll between bodies
that are not your own

on stainless steel tables
always the same question
unanswered

to understand life
by looking at death

6.

in the warped slipstream
of a cool beer
a lost son
and a long life

the days number themselves

pulling up the skin
like a fresh bedsheet
over a returning child

7.

in this east coast triangle
your daughters calculate the distance
between themselves → & you

a triangle can have two sides.

8.

closely watched
by your Panasonic Senate
of nine televisions

giant tinfoil barbs
in an 8ft aquarium
are still swimming
in your eyes

9.

this is not a pipe.

it's the reminiscence of a quiet boy
in his Gran's Greenslopes house
O-Cedar shine on wide pine boards
burnt-sugar notes in ritual residue in port-infused tobacco
as you tap out of mouth-cornered moments
strung together through your resonant voice
a little wary in its oak tone in a way
a match for the furniture sheen throughout
crafted by your father's hand
dead when you were thirteen
his name kept for the first grandson

the radiogram
with its art deco electrics
always a juke box
for silent tunes

the pipe a kind of pet
when called gladly absorbs itself
in your hand with absolute loyalty

the pipe
a portable incinerator
for unused thoughts

10.

he whispers himself
into his ear, though never hears
from himself
again

11.

in this unusual sleep
in which our difference
designs each other
heartbeats dissolve
drop by drop
into the same
glass

12.

one witness is skimmed from life.

one life is skimmed from memory.

it's rare for a mirror
to catch fire

rarer for someone
to see himself

but you clocked yourself

left a diamond on the windowsill
made from your patience
compressed

audiobooks for the dead

i.m. Rita & Joe St Ledger (1933/1934 – 2019/2022)

when God offers a choice
between the red and the white,

always take the red ←

thought bubbles in the blood
as simple as the o in other
we become the nest
in search of six eggs

veins laid straight
in a box labelled
'limitless forgiveness'

footsteps on the front lawn
permeate dirt under the fingernails
in clock hands

miniature rudders under open eyes
navigate gentle whirlpools in a moat
to protect bone bearers in a suburban castle
held in place by wooden hands
built on nothing other than → (memory)

the same stories at different times
are different stories at the same time
that multiply our organs ad infinitum
into a fermented air that never stops
teaching the lungs to impersonate clouds

monogrammed with hand-lettered punctuation
pulled back to earth with a shepherd's crook
which confesses Question Mark as its day job

in this house lemons glow unseen at night.

salt & pepper shakers sketch each other without expectation.

the fridge in open tuning hums an ecg jazz.

inside its walls ←
x-rays reveal a polite battalion of ladders
the family uses to climb up to the past
or down from the future

extra places are set at the table for our shadows.

we compare lists of all the books
that crawled into our beds
while we were sleeping

our irises in themselves are first editions.

hemming our way along the lips
of this inner-city ocean

on this side of the ledger
all the saints wear comfortable shoes

chalk lines around our feet
play hopscotch with death
welcoming it like any other stranger
as it drains unsalted tears
from our bank accounts

the e in end always smiling.

a waltz on water
hitched to the hips
of the river

nursery rhymes
eaten in the song
of a butcher bird

each generation
is reminded that a book
is a life

a box of bibles
strewn like lily-pads
across the surface of ART

avocet steps to nowhere
arrive unburdened by their weight
are acknowledged as prayers

this is the sound of labour
notating drops of sweat as they fall
on drumskin

nothing is more useful
than to look upon the world
as it really is, and at the same time
look elsewhere →

and (here) the counterbalance
of Irish humour sold by the bagful
in a not-for-profit existence

ALL of us experts in shaking laughter from a tree.

three points of contact
from the milking stool
that sends its roots into the ground

two interlocked commas
cast in undigested gold
nuzzle below their peat rug

why not let visions transcribe us for a change.

where basic words are left alone
to crawl off undulating margins
of their own choosing

we're still to perfect an envelope shape for the dream.

had they died
they would've lived
again

had they lived
they would've died
just once

just once
presence & absence
mourn each other

mirrors read aloud at sunset.

forget the silence until you are forgotten.

dark roads in white paint always take us home.

in a brick ark on a red hill
the times table can taste two bodies
on its tongue

paintings would return

for Gil Jamieson (1934–1992)

I.

paralleled by the manifesto
that he would be dead by 30
he continued to move away
from the categorisations of art
to art that always spoke for itself,
always urged people to reach
inside their own interpretations,
one to one, in landscapes
constantly wrestled with paint,
he found himself as a ten-year-old,
emphatically predicted to approach
figurative thought with subtle movement,
in a formulated tenor, doing National Service,
to acknowledge a myth, never prepared,
a rheumatic sketch surfaced among artists,
in nudes documenting political sincerity
following expectation into its sonnet family,
to farm Antipodean experience,

II.

he returned with grandiose plans,
and we set off again, to paint
a giant mirage, with both relationships
as a major influence, best displayed
in the killing he sought an escape from death,
to depict survival he painted raw truth,
and continued to exhibit there, in deep respect,
he returned to earlier times
because his mother was sick
because his mother commenced
a touring phase in his life,
commenced a close friendship
with famous art patrons, most impressed,
fishing for hard life over a waterhole
at Three Moon reflected upon the idea
first shown to exhibit cruelty,
he returned to exhibit 360° insanity
to depict both auctioneers after the sale,
exclusive drought dodgers from the coast
eating piglets on his land

III.

paintings would return as self-portraits
as his contemporaries were achieving
a remoteness from criticism, he consoled
himself on canvas, to try to start painting
again, after open-heart surgery,
after family tragedy, in 1985,
his mortality precipitated an intimate
association that never compromised
the non-second living near himself,
befriending himself, in the Five States,
that never sold readily, his second mortality,
again, managed to paint 30 self-portraits,
while he was hung in non-acknowledgement,
in a hospital with its archaeologist owner,
down south, a great supporter, down south,
to think a number received into himself
to receive art as himself into a number,
Bushman time dogmatic
about not being
Establishment time
in and around closer areas,
in and around the one representative,
in and around advanced diagnosis
he began travelling further
to move the cliff to the cancer
painting the education of time,
these paintings formed the new crop,
in great volumes producing song
in figurative oils never completed
his self-portraits bought themselves

in June 1992 in Monto
his self-portraits paint themselves
in Monto.

poems to dissolve on the skin

for Kathryn Roberts in memory of Ian Roberts (1938–2022)

I.

when someone
puts their arm through a sleeve
as if it's the next life

II.

can you explain
how you put a splint
on this echo

III.

it's true to say
you'll only cycle past yourself
once

IV.

cicadas undress
their January requiem
in his ears

V.

dream cars in a shipping container
under a toupée of gum leaves …
their headlights asleep

VI.

between the proverb and the parody
softening stones are thrown at pain
in a Glass House

VII.

three sisters
were carried into their own memory
by their father

VIII.

you said that grief is a bark overcoat
and we find ourselves and we lose ourselves
in its pockets

IX.

a silent bird without feathers
that unceasingly circles out of sight
yet never leaves your shoulder

X.

on twin peaks
your eyeballs adjust focus to film
one step in a timed life

XI.

and were you happy
with the way death pronounced
your name

XII.

one wall steps back in Hopetoun
to allow the other three
their masonry waltz

7th house

(Ariel,
Rocky,
Gordon,
Peter,
Jonathan,
Julie,
Isaak,)

molecule

for Ariel and Rocky Shepherdson

this is a thought molecule →

a constellation of points sculpturally reminiscent
of an Etruscan funerary figure

the black atoms are full stops

matter tailings compressed
into perfect negative space

but the composition
of its single red atom
is unknown

perhaps another transmitter
pared down from the same dot
on the same i in time that's travelled
every vein in all beings warm and cold

a lone detail
left to reshape itself to begin again
after distance is completely removed
from blood

this is a thought molecule ←

the object in this stick & ball game
where transcendent pharmacists and their loyal dogs alike
chase down alternate versions of their heads

to throw to
and for each

other

lure (Redland)

for Gordon Shepherdson

he throws his tongue
out the back of the boat
as a lure

sine wave protocols swim
in easy action in freedom and danger
as bait choreographs its invitation to be consumed
to be cleansed of all the words it once held
as speech

apostrophes in pursuit polish their scales
dart and disappear as sea-chrome messages
netted by the corners of our eyes
glint silver through codes we translate
as we blink

blue horses the size of your fingernail
pass themselves on the way to ordinary thought
where their manes are your eyelashes
bleached to perfect inoculation

he reminds us . . .

we're yet to record let alone capture
fragments of half-light that hitchhike
between chambers in the heart

we're in our daily commute through surface
through gravitational pores that stop our skin
becoming a balloon to be exploded by time

even a rainbow
after a squall is a measurement
in serene loneliness

a 7-strand lip
mute to its momentary
persuasion

we are described
by refracted hands that float mirrors
towards our rescue

he continues . . .

when i was a boy i hooked 80lbs of silence
and i'm still trying to reel it in

one day i'll realise i'm the creature on its line

as i hit the deck
as head and tail drum an end
through the ribs of a cast hull
where sound licks salt
into forgiving waters

in blood is every colour that isn't blood

the peace in your final sentence
is not what you think it'll be

if you read the tide as a lost bible
there's a small chance you'll believe
where you are

always trolling for the method
in the way the bay holds its breath

pH levels

for Peter Hudson

1.

those assembled
in the hall put up their hands and say,
'your portrait is not lost on me'

2.

this portrait
in an ambulance we made
for ourselves

3.

how the portrait sang
back at us without
any voice

4.

unnamed engineers arrive
to assess if the body will collapse
under its portrait

5.

at the restaurant
i ask for the bill and am given
my portrait

6.

they stood there for sixty years
to watch the bones fall out
of his portrait

7.

and the portraits protest
outside the museums of the world
for their subjects to be repatriated

Matt Colour (aka, the first shadow to stare down the sun)
for Jonathan McBurnie – 40th birthday

and how do you
pull four decades
into one day?

etch a different skull onto the same
hubcaps every time the wheel turns
as you cruise past your childhood
home with headlights OFF so as
not to wake the colour coding in
matchbook murals staring back at

you,

in high
definition

memory,

this is the first line you saw
before you knew
what it was

tossing seconds to the clock
like peanuts thrown in the air
to line up half-a-life later
to snap down your gullet
in an empty town square named
after Hermann Nitsch where
there are no statues dedicated
to those who sadly died of

choking,

this is not an answer
if this is not the question
even if those two words
even if those two words

say,

otherwise,

and what's to be unlocked
when the volume in the body
is NOT discernible except to
those who paint their stones
RED before pegging them at
passersby?

sososo
so   so
sososo,

don't quote the wall when IT says

'ART preserves what it destroys'

after all,

a prayer is just
a single clap
you won't

hear,

this is the space
in the poem where
you get to → insert
your own text into
a lost film

OR,

finally use the gift voucher
that entitles you to take your
first skydiving lesson into
blind theory

sososo
so   so
sososo,

around the corner

down the hill

just up here

you'll come across
a temperature-controlled room
sighing at 19 degrees

inside the
room will

BE,

a million fresh cumquats
stacked in pyramid form
with a lipstick equator on

each no doubt telling you
that as a colour OR-ange
is considered OFF limits
even though the one at the
summit the one skiing your
squint that one cumquat
is somehow monogrammed
with your

initials,

sososo

so   so

sososo,

is the radiation
in diseased laughter
still funny?

can all the ceilings in this town
fold themselves into appropriate
pockets in inappropriate ways
before nightfall?

if form follows function
then where do we follow
our bodies to when our
shadows forget to return
their rented suits?

femurs for toothpicks
saddle the hip replacement
in your thinking

the mirror always knew
how to body slam your being
without breaking itself

wrestlers become pall bearers
in the maternity ward when you
wake up with a conceptual
spoon in your

mouth,

are these the same things
you'd draw if you didn't
have a

hand,

in a kind of walk-sign silhouette
you stand like a grenadier in a
loud shirt as you film surveyors
staking out acres of bruised flesh
Splovero-style to inwardly catch the
canula-hup-2-3-4 blood pricks on
300 mctre

arms,

sososo
so   so
sososo,

is this surface the planar parody
assembled in documentary quicksand
clogging heart valves in another
suburban tragedy?

the trick with simplicity
is working out how to bake
a glass key into the eye

yesterday,

you read an article
recounting how surgeons now use
equals signs to staple the skin

tomorrow,

you might decide to order a scalpel
guaranteed to dance like Martha Graham
as her toenails cut Anaximander's sole passage
into your

back,

now you now use
equals signs to staple
your skin

sososo
so   so
sososo,

did your drawing relinquish
its lines to either object or figure
or was it the other way

round,

your pen nibs swimming with the weight
of 1200 mullet are soon netted
in the page

as another vial of ink
is talked down off another granite ledge
in epigrammatic perspective

and you'll notice the windows
they've pulled out of your chest
over the years are all stacked
neatly along the back

wall,

the ball bearings you planted
in the front yard as a child
ensure your ecclesial supply
of hand-milled chrome

lozenger metals
you permit your body
to suck on like the first

rib,

On what iOns
and in what cOlOur
did yOu skate yOur tOngue
tO the Other end Of the

table,

(even an uneven table
has to wait to be asked
to sit down)

and did your tongue break
its silence more than once
or break your silence once

more,

or did your tongue
just say nothing as usual
before it flopped open to reveal
a pearl the size of a

cumquat,

sososo
so   so
sososo,

the banks of the river
foreclose yet again on
the overdrawn eyes of
their customers

the blood on the apron
of the butcher was your
confession even though
he said he would bring y
our heart back

,

this ← is the only question
you can ever ask
yourself

the one still asleep
in your third
lung

this painting taught me about the dangers of horizontals

for Julie Fragar

which hand
would painters use if they
didn't have one

which painting
puts a window to sleep
by being the rock that
leaves a perfect hole
in its glass

the bodies in the surface
are not always the ones
actually there

the bodies on the surface
are as (close) as all
distancecombined

is the democracy in
the surface the same
thunder nailed into a
postage stamp on the
letter you sent to
Marlene

sneaking your body parts out
in fresh loaves of bread

black butter as a
beauty treatment for
the dry bed in an
empty lake

(it says so on the
back of the pack)

this means there is no river
we can cry each other into
but we can still pick up the
current inside hems knotted
in memory at crossroads that
softly transmute us into
untroubled light

when somebody says,
'skin is the only word
with an i in it'→ nobody
disagrees

basically art's about having
the wherewithal to stand in
the dinghy → in that Shelley
Winters moment → then drop
the cloth as your signal → having
arranged to torpedo yourself ←

consequence finds new playmates
by killing its fresh litter of ideas
each morning

dripped signatures from unknown
hands unable to read the backs of
themselves are served with ice
for our chosen authenticators

dogs that don't bark
whisper in bone code

Unheard.

Unhear.
Unher.
Unhe.

Un.
U.
.

(there's your meditative still
life for the day offering its
profound observations
as to why it left
its vase)

colour can't escape its silence

colour beat the heart
into the first
readymade

and we've all heard the stories
about painters stuffing art history
into a stockinette to drag along
the shoreline at low tide to
pull bloodworms straight
out of blank canvas

but now it's
diffferent

but now it's
diffferent

no more Bauhaus wallpaper
under the armpits
for hair removal

no more manifestos
desperate to talk Adam
into abandoning the first
syllable

town planners in suede
overcoats vow never
to stop jogging until they can
run through the museum
without walls while imploring
artists to put down their brushes
with a similar compunction to vets
putting down either horses or
forgotten painters on race day

you show me the new
instrument you bought
online for measuring the
blood loss in a concept

or for beginners there's
always the pinhole camera
as a secondary universe
where brush handles keep
sprouting leaves

angles without sleep
are the straight lines
to be hung
onto,

then,
there's the other head

the one that fits inside
a boxing glove as easy
as truth auctioning teeth

the one you get to segment like a
POrtuguese OR-range where cortex
slices invite marination or even
mandatory entry into the long held
biannual Pessoa Nomenclature Quiz
where you have less than a minute to
recite all his pseudonyms while eating
one segment of OR-range between each
name is the only name they won't
allow you to say

at least on your own you
can recognise the shared
functionality of your body
as it swings in a hammock
strung between the warm
epiglottides of your parents

was the way forward
the way back
to there

??? ??? ??? ???????
??? ??? ????
?? ??ere

and in your opening address
each year you sometimes posit,,,

what's the difference between
Art & Remorse?

only one of them has
fingerprints but no one
knows which one yet both
can detect either even if
neither of them is there

(no one ever laughs although
you think it's funny anyway)

isn't irony the boat
they used to bail out
the bucket

the same wood is
used whether you're
asked to make a chair
or an answer

and is it you or your patience
wearing thin as you listen
to the dissertation on how
long it takes to cook the deer
in headlights with the primary
constraint that only the light
from the headlights can be
used to cook
the deer

what we carry delivers us

sends context to an upholsterer
to be restuffed with shadows

the accuracy of the scales
you use to weigh images
has been checked although
a comment was noted that
they looked remarkably like
your eyes

was the way back
the way forward
to here

??? ??? ??? ????
??? ??? ???????
?? ?ere

this is you ←

giving a standard example
of biochromatic downsizing
of the soul into alien dust
searching for divine approval
on its aesthetic mortgage

this is you →

as you demonstrate how
to swim towards a brain
in hot soup

this is how it'll work,,,

Fontana leaves the knife in
the canvas for Gentileschi to
leave the knife for Judith to
leave in Holofernes' neck

and once that's done
you'll have to come up
with a slogan to paint
on a travertine floor

'on a diet of lost ankles
we walk to ourselves'

Fred MacMurray leaves 3 unanswered messages for himself

for Isaak Shepherdson

Alexander Zverev
(Sascha) ←

when the lines on the court
move through softshell judgements
recounted in the requiem of the long-night
for the featherless owl,   ,

kids giggle at random points
in the crowd, slightly open
matchboxes they found in the carpark
to listen to dissident screams they'll
never hear, to close them with delight
at the prize, before the umpire caresses
the microphone as a truncheon
for quiet

splayed-foot shuffle to the bassline, slight
stoop, hips relaxed, something in the crease
of your eye that unfolds into mine, that
unfolds into both eyes of a squinting son,
collecting five years from unleavened distance,
as you turn, take your stance, ready to serve
into the wind, you notice the Holzer-typo
in a red prayer rolling across the scoreboard,
the whole surface now water, your body
wrapped in the net on the floor of the river
Elbe, your hair blonde algae, your gold chain

locked in glint comparison
with silver perch,

you still win the match.

↓

●

↓

my goal in this, is
simply to remember
that you have skin

what if we just sat
on wooden chairs at either end
of an ant bed court?

do you think
the chairs would speak
first?

you know our silence
has the same
shoe size?

the lisps we don't have,
we are yet to encounter,
by accident

fish roe inside the tongue
ready to translate fingerlings
into words

one conversation could uproot
the trees in our throats,
you think?

here are the two ghosts
i'd like you to meet
(   ) (   )

polar icecaps in a scotch glass
drink a world drained away
from us

this is the gauge
to detect rising sea levels
between two people

at least once a day,
sometimes more, i speak
your name to the breeze

fascinated to watch
an eagle carry two hearts
to its nest

jotting time, observations,
wondering when they'll hatch
into versions of ourselves

we are the two ghosts
i'd like you to meet
(   ) (   )

kicking a ball
to each other from
separate cages

at night, pulling our webs
into strange shapes, from opposite
corners of the same skylight

on the back of the bottle,
it says to add two drops of absence
to our coffee, twice a day

„ „ „
„ „ „

on a limewash wall, we hang naked
from titanium hooks under our collar
bones, the difference in age of the body
type is noted but similarities persist to
the fact the two figures must be related,
saliva codes sent as a chorus to remove
handles from speech (again), what say
you, as fingerprints on wings as mites
to the eye, our toes buoyant in air
commence incremental growth to
ground, under an arraignment
of cloud and compassion,
we mouth the other's
name

„ „ „
„ „

Toby Wallace
(Moses) ←

when an angel
climbs out of the drain,
you offer him a chair.

crows on the fence
look over their sunglasses
like paperback Lolitas.

a good body in a bad shirt blows
the numbers off a roulette wheel,
stinks more shadows to sweat, as your
membership card dissolves into a balloon
crammed with a Smarties®-pack of pills,
arrives like a letterbox wearing Vans®, to let
you know your clown-hood ways have been
recognised, and that you have permission to
tend the graves of those you love, until you
find yourself
in one.

your chaos is the fuel that walks
crumbs up the table leg back to the plate
where the cake is absent but well dressed
by the stomachs of those you've only just
met, those who will mean more to you than
any life-changing event could possibly offer,
where truth is sprayed on like repellent, then
washed off like shipwrecked souls in a backyard
pool where words on a cheekbone, words
behind your ear, keep your head
afloat.

the meat-prong with which
you never threatened anyone,
still, in a drawer at your grandad's
house.

↓

■

↓

can you send me the forwarding address
for your father's memory?

we've got an endless supply of clover,
laser-cut from granite
in search of its luck

black spots on the lung explode
as bombers fly over an open field
where we both lie, open-mouthed,
parachutes on our teeth, for when
they land on the surface of Mars,
hymns at the ready for infinite silence,
tongue-tip counting pulled pins under
obsolete lips unwed from gravity are
the grenades we swallow in turn, to
save one from the other, to relinquish
one for the other, eyelids salted, cured,
ham-sliced off unechoing faces of forgotten
gods who were never the recipients of even
one prayer, let alone birdseed held open-palm
as an offering for the betterment of all things,

or perhaps just two genetically ticked beings
who hope to stand either side
of the same door.

is it possible
that the music in your hands
can remove the fingerprints
from your mirror
to leave them
on mine?

neon gas in my veins
trains itself to cursive script,
your name aflicker on my forearms,
across my chest, along my calves,
sentient devotion, stripped of its
fat, bandaged transparent in one
unending thought.

is it possible
to work out how to use
our faces as signal lamps,
edit light from one bridge to another,
reduce a language entire, to what
we need to say, before steel bows kiss,
and fathoms pull our hulls downward
with the speed of lead hands, encrusted
in blind salt.

and if we find ourselves.

(yet not with each other).

in a room with twelve chairs,
knowing one of those chairs is not real,
one of those chairs is solidified shadow,
has the look, the weight, the feel, of the real
thing, and we get one chance to pick it, one
chance to put every breath, future or past, into
one choice, and if we get it right, ask of ourselves
the only question to be answered, as likely as bending
the knees in a stone, we'll sit down, our bodies matchheads
to the tongue of a solar flare that whips us
back to earth.

one stilted blink
to adjust before we look
at each other.

Dan DeHaan
(Chris) ←

even your watch looks away.

timpani thud repeats a split watermelon smile
with the back of your skull, prospector's licence
to look for blood on concrete, Rorschach-red,
it rains one life away, miniature tsunami edging
a new shore away from brutal quiet, as if Hepworth
had been given a Prometheus liver to play with,
for one day,

the character replaces the actor, the
actor replaces himself, with you, in
my head, blood still on the stove, a
projectionist's lunch, soup stirred with
a wooden spoon, into memory, it lets go
of the image it can never leave, until
the sky is another doorbell, until you're
gone, i won't be there, mistaking loss
for alacrity, mincing willow-tree hands
into the mute scream, chisel to the
shinbone to keep me
walking,

eye whites a curious mix
of polished quartz
and lemon pith

red splatter effect
from your sinus nodes
as spray gun

in the parallel parade of decoys,
we pick out each other
with one glance,

cue tip to the white ball,
the angular adage, that the
first look is the best shot,

↓

▲

↓

i give you my fingernails
in a cigar box.

you tell me there's one
missing.

in turn, you leave two dog-eared
boxes at the end of my bed, ask
me to put everything i've done
into one, and put everything i haven't
done, into the other

i ask, how I can tell
the difference?

'ich, ich und meine Sünden,
die sich wie Körnlein finden
des Sendes an dem Meer,'

others say, 'he'll come round,'

i ask for the address of absence?

we should show each other
the carry bags for our skulls
our mothers made us

large praying mantis nests
with a shoulder strap, they'll
convert into lanterns
when we're born

eyes on a pickle fork
donated to a museum set up
to outline the history
of blinking

a new function of meteorology
to predict the temperature
of blood

'Erwäge,

wie sein blutgefärbter Rücken
in allen Stücken dem Himmel
gleiche geht.'

and, do your hands get tired
counting his breaths?

miraculous blue pollen
unsteady in stone lungs

i say your name
to breathe it
back in

lips nailed to the fence posts
of liars are reused to save the lives
of those who can't
speak

when asked to define loneliness
they all draw freehand shapes
and point to the line

most words die before they're born,
leave their punctuation uncut
in sun-raked marble

a tongue
the first fossil
in any language

the easiest way
to detect sleep
is by its laugh

the two small dogs
waiting to be fed, in
the family home,
are us

when we're ready,
we won't be there

stars break as easily
as a wineglass under aim
from the universal aria
we can't hear

one spade
into soft ground
severs the neck

.

,

8th house

(Ann,
Sandra,)

What the Painter is Told on the Subject of Landscape
for Ann Thomson

, have you ever seen air bleed,

, stuffed a cloud like a white hanky
in the bolt-hole in your hand,

, i'm not talking rain or wind, i'm talking an incision,
a mile high, the width of a hair,
whale-hunt red,

, one long stitch, shoulder height,
ankle deep, worn like a choroid Mackintosh
by an atmosphere checking passports in refugee light,
that'll pass through it, through itself, again,
in a radium fist-clench, as self-appointed
protector to the one touch
bent into all colour,

, did the water wait for you to wait for it,

, and when you say, 'you
threw away the horizon
a long time ago',

, did you realise
you are the horizon
when you lie down,

, as safe as houses never built
because the architect's ribs couldn't
drum up enough strength to cut
through the pinstripes on his
waistcoat,

, did you realise there's footage
of you cleaning between your teeth
with an Olivetti® typewriter ribbon,

, magneto rhythms protest outside your eyes,

, stain the legible with what it means to be the stain,

, is this the need ← to keep what you forget →,

, where you're asked to turn the page
in the bookseller's dream, thoughts squeezed
from piano felt, as you paint over his forehead,
over his forehead, until it falls off in your
hands,

, this is the soup spoon dipped in sunlight
in an upturned skull that will soon hover back
to your mouth,

, the weight in everything is the weight in time,

, a wooden chair floating in
open ocean, translucent tentacles
in a closed-eye sway, politely seats the
daguerreotype dossier left by your
mother's face,

, it's pretty simple, isn't it, it's
pretty simple, isn't it, how your
fingerprints drift to nowhere
after heavy rain,

, you just wander through doors that aren't there,

, watch another video on how to lay
turf on your back so you can finally
walk to the letterbox,

, the wait in everything is the wait in time,

, amazing that you can use a bridge for a hairpin,

, a drawing close to the perfect milking machine for memory,

, shoelaces around your wrists
remind you to walk home
on your hands,

, Dorothy taught you the way
round the object was also the
way through it,

, and this is an example of Passmore wicker,
modelled on the interlocked fingers of Cezanne,
a waterproof cane once popular in post-impressionist
gardens, it was used to make traps for octopus, or young
artists, who adhered to the lifelong study in the use of
green,

, an urgent call was put in for a Fairweather kiss,
picked up somewhere on the silk road, haunted, never
quite at home, in snaking calligraphic blue, it accepts
the stolen cheekbones of hydrangeas, the subject
reports back that his Bribie-beard
is still growing,

                                  , your back now against the bus window
                                      in morning sun irons your skin
                                            like a fresh tablecloth,

, yellow sound inside mottled eggs
flattened the nest you didn't notice,

                          , just stand there until you disappear →,

, only drink the outline of your shadow ← cold,

                              , scrape out the eyelids of the Colossus,
                          use them as oven mitts, wash them in brine,
                                        stick'em in a painting,

, they only just managed
to close the doors of a carriage
stuffed with feathers.

                                  , = bird carcasses line the tracks =,

, there's always a place in the queue
for witnesses who wished they'd committed
the crime,

                  , they decide to oust the government to vote for the lies,

, this is a photo of Ann leaping,

, sand in the eye of everyone known
was swept aside by the accountant
of solitary visions,

, no cannonball-in-the-stomach-act
in the same circus that sells off the
bits of your life you paint to stay
alive,

, in this catacomb for suspended energy
whole continents glow on the scale
of a pinhead,

, too many barking equations in shadows that need to be fed,

, the small chaos in perfect fruit that falls
the length of a lightyear to predecease itself
in intricate patterns charged with remembering
infinity as a galactic psalm,

, you've never met a candle that believed it was on fire,

, arcs in firehose form are assessed for reflex fitness,

, loose scars in a tin trunk reused
to mend fishing nets, pull holes back to
rhizome squares where mermaids have bitten through
art history,

, waiters in Prussian blue aprons are refused entry to the studio,

, this is a photo of Ann leaping,

, when she lands colour will explode,
bare feet the trip-switch for the depth charge, a
half-gurgle of physics on a surface that just manages
to repel or embrace an aesthetics in total collapse,
convincing what's left to stay in a 360 realm thanks to tent pegs
punched through canvas at 90 degrees teaching an unruly
prism the obedience of sitting on its
wall,

, sometimes you're fortunate enough to see the windchimes ignite,

, sometimes the mirror trusts you enough to recognise
that you won't recognise yourself,

, the N and the N,
like Japanese clogs, woodblock sounds
as you walk away from yourself towards another
modern composition to conduct distance at close
quarters when half the time you're someone
else,

, the O and the O,
a pillory pair stuck in a visual
click-track, where your hands are
captured then released, captured then
released by the counting patterns in each
breath, the counted pebbles in one
being, alone, a lung forming itself in
a wave rolling out from a dissolving
shore,

, head still at the point of contact,

, tarpaper assumes the role of your
skin turned inside out, the bitumen-run in
petrochemical tears oozed from mantle and marrow
into the violent safety of studio light,

, sloop renditions in drowned applause,

, the many arguments with many selves
where only the lighthouse-keeper is permitted
to rule on the debate,

, unsteady hearts shot
like enamel-black basketballs
off the Sydney Heads,

, where they land
is where they
came from,

, heads without buttons
push the buttons
without heads,

, if a clay pigeon is context then speech is the gun,

, the bulk cargo in language mostly
condemned to description, yet there is a handful
of words unable to describe, unable to describe
unable, that never surrender
their atomic weight,

, lips descend like snowflakes in totalitarian speech,

, even rumours will celebrate a significant birthday,

, more unscented ovations
that now understand why you
kept what you forgot,

, you are told the three-and-a-half
words you need to remember when
silence tries to plot your discourse
with a well-timed hole in the
ground,

, is this the type of shadow
you grate over porridge
in winter,

, where head-wrapped contrast arranges
to meet itself beneath the nail on your right
index finger to re-draft the treaty between
things-life & things-death, boiled down to suet,
onto the single-white-page-as-metaphor for bone
degeneration, inevitable but unconcerned by more
words that were never left on the page
(alone),

, is this the celestial tuning
of gold screws being caught
in a bell,

, is this your subconscious proficiency
in rubber-tapping colour
from botanical time,

, the NOTHING that lands on the railing
while you sip a coffee, the NOTHING that
expects to be thrown softened bits from a
Brisbane mirror,

, you say you said,

, 'the sea in one glass
drank us all, stirred
our bodies with silver
lightning from a
teaspoon',

, windows turn to smoke
before your eyes
turn to flame,

, gravity complains its shoes are uncomfortable,

, you think you thought,

, what we return to returns to us,

, the scream without vocal cords the purest prayer,

, did anything else happen in 1933,

, ghosts continue to use your ears
as pedal-boats in a fun park, moments
away from liquidation,

, the trauma in the question
unable to relax until the perfect
invitation is received,

, INCIDENT RESPONSE,

, INCIDENT RESPONSE,

, ←,

, →,

, the blue-sky mumble in truth,

salt

for Sandra Selig

silence always loosens time.

these heads were formed without bone.

unmatched hands in oblivion
smear echoes out of cellular plasticene
as skin

this shoreline lipped
to the saxophone's mouth
sends postcards to the lungs

sound that prowls with its welcome

an aural chiropractor for lost thought

the brass smirk in an old riddle
about capturing sound
by letting it go

one day

they'll bend the saxophone
into an ampersand

raise it as proof
wordbound to respirated energy
Zungenruder in co2 tuning

and you'll be the first
to play it

a conjunction of personal galaxies

feathers instead of lashes
over your eyes closed
in their nest orbiting
as patient as unhatched time

long forgotten

just remembered

every switch on the wall
a new tongue apprenticed to the dictation
of light multiplied in elastic ozone
coiled gently around your ears
where vagrants sleep peacefully
under the ledge of their doomed equation
still guaranteed to hold its answer
until we accept that within every mirror
is the invitation to lie down in its frame
to accept that every face is your own
but each body belongs to another
in our first undressing from the womb
names can only stare at spaces
between letters and frown at the fact
that if meaning can already stand

then why can't i

◘

did we not speak without words.

leave our syllables limbless
on a causeway before the dream
was challenged to open its eyes

in speech are all the words
i will never borrow

a prayer unmentioned is never said
to be more concise than the one
already uttered

i would never shoot an arrow
that had not been withdrawn
from my flesh

never light a candle
until you tell me your fingers
are bloomed wicks

in speech are all the words
that will borrow you

in our inherited oven
baked stones are always
ready to eat

(as)

you predict
the universe will dissolve
when confronted with itself

(our little joke to tickle dark matter)

full stops in a collection plate
far heavier than the god
to which they were donated

the people we see
will only issue arrest warrants
if they see us (together)
in our rubber boots

steady rain talks
to its design before falling
into cupped hands

we have never heard anyone
yell at the sea
to shut up

◼

above the triangle of a dirty roof
an ibis flies south and a crow flies east
black away from white in a primary separation
of colour where wings (of course) stabilise the air
to massage a glid momentum we unfailingly watch
through the grime-grid of a screen door
somehow jealous when insects feel obliged
to breach the idea of its other side
where you sit with half-cold coffee
on a kitchen chair with split upholstery
that always guessed the correct weight
of my father's best thoughts   (   )

to which i would say;;

'stairs sometimes need to be disassembled
at night, as an acceptable substitute for a
pillow, if you ever expect to walk anywhere
without moving.'

to which you would say;;

anything

can

swim

in

either

.

everything

drowns

in

or

.

the living & the dead
carry each other ashore
on this island we call *Else*

members in your private senate
ankle-deep in sand ask to take turns
reading placards in your memory

belt buckles
picked from unleavened ash
are made into new belts

flute-squeal-cuts
appear in birch bark
in an Austrian hometown

note the dry ice gap-pinch our shoulder blades
as our full names are scribbled
in the margins of the next deluge

◘

we track the evening brown
whisper its exit through a studio door
onto a solitary leaf
that has never been
for sale

trees in the shape of song
prepare their egos
for take-off

a casuarina needle
with its nose and tail in a wall
becomes a walking stick for shadows

tension defined in its dozen or so elbows
enlisted by newfound form
as a haiku curve

you overhear you

say

'the earth is obedient
provided you follow through
with your promise
to make it square.'

i overhear me

say

'i resolve nothing
by being
alive.'

dark matter to dark hum
our for binge-drinking p
hysicists in paper bombe
r jackets and muddy snea
kers who fantasise about
knocking a hole in the ne
arest star to dive through
it like six-year-old acroba
ts in training then consu
ming it as the giant doug

hnut it is covered in a ligh
tyear's worth of saturny
sugar

so you
see so
you se
e so yo
u see

i become unruly when i talk to trees

chop my legs off to expose nesting parrots
plumage inevitably red petitioning to be blue
or mauve through the unnecessary counteroffers
all said and done in contractual black

in the parliament of the littoral why

tertiary sunshine lists
in this chartered vessel
of eternal departure

◘

for years i've watched you map folds in the memory.

tear elegance
out of its socket
without the pain

recitative ↔ recitative
recitative ↔ recitative
recitative ↔ recitative

a kind of rhumba
in the unexplained static
from an object yet to breathe

from these half declamations
yet to be received yet to be read
in your telegrams for comets

(stop)

the rock above your head
is the same as the rock
beneath your feet except
your feet are above
your head above the
rock

(stop)

surgery is being performed
as we speak to remove the anxiety
from all rumour

(stop)

warped timber a giant hair comb
lost by a priestess from that other world
trapped in its velvet cocoon

(stop)

the songvoice inside bamboo
can wash behind the ears
of any soul

(stop)

you are not allowed
to mention the moon
inside its circle un° less°
the moon mentions
you

(stop)

in response to the question

we decide instead to undress
the window in ourselves

(stop)

this camel as its own constellation
finally repairs the unassailable rip
in our sky

(stop)

the wind does not tire
of drawing self portraits

(stop)

the cameras used to photograph
ghosts are the ghosts

(stop)

no spider has ever failed maths

(stop)

◧

the lines you draw are not from your hand.

we all watch you demonstrate
how to take the blood pressure
of rolled steel

to salt
the body
is impure

as an artist you eat
your subject

what is empty is full.

it's easy to say

(listen)

(   )

what is empty is full.

(   )

where do you put the absence
once removed

how do you store the absence
twice remembered

is the idea of salt
in and of itself enough

for preservation

did the swallows recognise their flight path

regale your passerine self
with stories of bearded mathematicians
cutting open their eyeballs
hoping to retrace the patterns
within

cone to the pendulum

cut to the push

you set free corrosive hope
through a missing apex that
will not find its fingertip again
as a nozzle-sway in an air-dance
perhaps seven minutes is long enough
longer than the single vertical
of its egg-timing cousin pulling
geometric gauze from cutaway

nautilus-andromeda patterns willing
to search for us as witnesses seeking
permission for our skin to be dust
we realise we won't make it to the
altar where numbers are used instead
of incense and gravity is used instead
of words in this ceremony that cannot
take place until it ends unrecognised
as having been here at all our bones go
from feather to clay to smoke to secrets
held aloft in these colour-helm refractions
given off evaporative saliva last lisp to first
mirror in this espionage in space that tells us
to forget who we are but to record even cherish
indeed promote where we're from even if it doesn't
exist.

if it doesn't exist

we do.

(   )

(   ).

o,
kay,,,

i confess
i stole
this pillar of salt
from the bible

i returned it
as a perfect cubic metre of meat
resting on a glass floor
where footfalls unend
in deaf chance

i was looking
to rust your toenails
to offer ceaselessness
to the magnet
on which
you stand

observing

your inverted homage to thirst.

your salt glissando minus its sea.

your sodium-white trellis
on which cornered light will grow
towards glistened teeth belonging
to your crystal judge

the rust releases its damaged prayers
into chemistry inhospitable to the touch
it produces fingerprints (not from your hand)
big enough to convict our insignificance

no art was committed in the making of this crime.

all crime is committed to emancipate this art.

do not trust a wound you didn't make.

leave the future behind.

the broom
easily translates the language
in your feet

◘

all   this   before

all   this   before

all   this   before

( )   ( )   (   )

the forgotten present ←
at the back of the cupboard
you were given when you were (8)

uranium-soaked mallets
you will use to play the fontanelle plates
in a bear's head

this is our opportunity to lie
open-mouthed under lemniscate forms
dripping compound truths

trinket grammar
collapsed over wine-pressed gravesides
where only lips can be interred

despite the infinite
there are only three numbers
on time

helium tastebuds
steam themselves up
from clock compost

sentences received with eyelids closed

with what you ask
is what i am
told

(and)

in every three-legged race
is the greying dog that unburied the heart
she left at your feet

(and)

we are told we will be
the first two to be killed
by the sound of a slamming door

◘

i was not asleep until you woke me.

notes

Epigraph from *The Lemon House* by Luca Pescatore (*L'eterno Squalo - Selected Poems 1960–2003*, Certaldo Alto Editore, 2013). Translation by Marco Ridi.

teacher – the last line a refers to the aria *Ombra mai fù* in Handel's opera *Xerxes*.

whiting 36 × 36 – 2021 oil on linen by John Honeywill.

liturgy in llama land – 'your husband' refers to Laurence McGuckin (1930–2012); 'your son' refers to Justin McGuckin (1961–2022).

framing references until the walls complain – this sequence is a non-ekphrastic response to Anne Wallace's 2020 survey exhibition *Strange Ways* at QUT. The poems grew from and orbit out of the Greenslopes / Holland Park locale. In **satisfactions** – E.P. Trewern (1895–1959) – Brisbane architect. In **Greenslopes** – John Heywood died in a site accident in 1934 in part of the factory complex designed by E.P. Trewern. My grandmother Muriel Portley (1901–1988) lived directly behind the abandoned factory.

lips over a waterfall is an award commission from the Sophia Nugent-Siegal Estate. This award commenced in 2018. Sophia was a gifted poet, science fiction writer, and ancient historian from Maleny in Queensland. Other recipients of the award to date are MTC Cronin, Alice Oswald, David Musgrave, and Paul Kingsnorth. Thank you to Robyn Nugent for the invitation to create this work.

BIVT (10/40) is drawn from Samuel Beckett's 1974 poem *Something There*. BIVT = Beckett Intravenous Vowel Transfer. The vowels have been mapped from their original positions in Beckett's poem.

an object may undo itself – after *Wind Sequence (16 seconds) no. 1*, 2015, by Arryn Snowball.

penneggiole – a local dialect word from the San Gimignano region for the saffron milk cap mushroom (*lactarius deiliciosus*).

reefwalkers - This suite of found poems was constructed using *CORALS of the GREAT BARRIER REEF* by Ern Grant (born 1924), published by E.M. GRANT PTY. LIMITED, Scarborough, 1991. The 'found' method used in these poems is to slice, splice, and transfer phrases and words as they exist from the original text. Capitalisations and punctuation have been preserved as is. This work is a coda piece to *Slack Water*, a book-length collaboration of art and poetry made with Arryn Snowball. The Grant family mounted a display of 1840 hand-tinted corals at Expo 1967 in Montreal. (the extra t in setttle may allow a view of Golgotha in lower case.)

EMG
MEG

letter torque – these poems were written in response to a new font Aalphabet created by Aaron Perkins. Aaron has kindly set these poems in that font elsewhere.

hamartiologist board game – a simple grid. 26 × 26. Each blank space is a letter. Each word is scrambled. The spaces are read in the horizontal. Where a word contains a letter more than once, the blank space forms a vertical with the line below. In the initial, the reader is asked to construct each poem as intended by the poet. However, experimentation is encouraged. Special thanks to Anna Jacobson as test pilot. Answers: 1. when asked to open his mouth he said he was his mouth bar the yawning / 2. using the tongue to paint skin on every wall until every body you require is there / 3. with feathers dipped in mercury you became the mirror to become the god / 4. another cocktail for the lost time garnished with lab grown hearts on toothpicks / 5. fingers in the font for Judas as the first investment banker / 6. a fresh delivery of eyelids on the lawn you will not bother to open / 7. your own recipe for jerky for all the ears you were forced to cut off

indelible watermark for birth certificates – the comma spacings are the product of a long succession of coin tosses. Heads = 1 space, Tails = 2 spaces. Thanks to QE II and the echidna. Coin design by Stuart Devlin. Coin used was minted in 2001. (not all commas are the fatted calves you imagine.)

library for paper tongues – the nun is a reference to the artist/poet Ōtagaki Rengetsu (1791–1875).

standing – 2020 sculpture by Lincoln Austin, located at Tulmur Place, Ipswich.

colour slides – in poem 6., the 'lost son', and poem 9., 'first grandson' refers to my cousin Mick Portley (1957–2013).

audiobooks for the dead – the stanza that begins *'nothing is more useful'* is from the encyclical by Pope Leo XIII. This passage was read at the funeral mass for Joe St Ledger.

paintings would return – is a found poem created from Matthew Jamieson's essay on his father Gil Jamieson, *A Painter of the Land*. (*Life on the Land* – Rockhampton Regional Gallery 1997). The essay was written with input by Alicia Jamieson.

lure (Redland) – a piece written as part of the opening address for my father's 2023 exhibition *Ocean of Eyes* at the Redland Art Gallery.

this painting taught me about the dangers of horizontals – the poem title is a quote by Julie Fragar from an artist's talk at the University of Sunshine Coast 15th April 2023. Julie was referring to her work, *This is Not a Dress Rehearsal: A Catalogue of Final Options* 2019. 'Marlene' refers to the South African painter Marlene Dumas (born 1953). 'Shelly Winters' is a reference to the 1951 film *A Place in the Sun*.

Fred MacMurray leaves 3 unanswered messages for himself – Alexander Zverev, born 1997, tennis player, known as Sascha. Toby Wallace, born 1995, actor, played Moses in *Babyteeth* (2019). Dane De Haan, born 1986, actor, played Chris Lynwood in *Zero Zero Zero* (2020). Stanzas in German are from the St John Passion by JS Bach. Fred MacMurray played Steve Douglas in the sitcom *My Three Sons* (1960–1972).

What the Painter is Told on the Subject of Landscape – the poem title is taken from a 2003 painting by Ann Thomson. 'Dorothy' refers to UK/NZ/Aust artist Dorothy Thornhill (1910–1987).

salt – this poem is a direct + indirect response to Sandra Selig's exhibition *Exploring Giant Molecules*, University of the Sunshine Coast 2022. *Zungenruder* = tongue rudder.

acknowledgements

soft meteorites was written either side of the Brisbane River (Maiwar) on Turrbal and Jagera country. I pay respects to elders past, present and emerging, acknowledging the creative spirits and beings of the land and waters.

Many thanks to family and friends for their continued interest, support, and on-going conversation. Reiterated thanks to all dedicatees of the poems (solid or in aether). On a personal level, I would like to offer extended thanks to Eve Fraser, Ariel Shepherdson, Isaak Shepherdson, Luke Shepherdson, Valerie Portley, Julie Portley, Catherine Portley, Lisa & Gerard O'Connell, Elizabeth & Robert McCray & family, Robyn Nugent, the St Ledger clan (in laws & outlaws), Morgan Grant & family, Pascalle Burton, Anna Jacobson, Margie Cronin, Tom Shapcott, Aidan Coleman, David Stavanger, Elisa Biagini, Nick Powell, Matt Hetherington, Jane Frank, Melinda Smith, Arryn Snowball, Megan Williams, Sandra Selig, Hamish Sawyer, Josh Milani, D Harding, Rowan Donovan, Bruce & Kathryn Heiser, Nerida Cooley, The Jamiesons, Louise Martin-Chew, Philip Bacon, Celie Forbes, Bruce Reynolds, Mr E, Ian Friend, Jan Manton, Kahl Monticone, Angela Gardner, Simone Gelli, Sandra Cesani, Kathryn Roberts, Kylie Spear, Robert Ashdown, Leighton Craig & Patrida Blake, Marco Ridi & Lisa Bonini, Tiffany & Kylie Johnson, Charlie Moore, Victoria Goring, Cahle Comer, and Steve Pearce.

Special thanks to Marian Drew for permission to use *Everything was more vivid* 2023, on the cover. (asleep in her lexicon with the speed of light). Image courtesy of the artist and onespace gallery.

Continued editorial thanks to Felicity Plunkett for her ability to tweezer the dot onto the letter i. (our crazy enterprise to try and find the light switch in every second.)

Thank you to the typesetter Keith Feltham for laying down the font-lines, allowing the handcar such easy passage between sentences. (can we move a full stop without the page noticing?)

Fully sculpted thanks to Terri-ann White at Upswell Publishing. We farm words in hope of being harvested by them. All we can do. I'm very fortunate to be offered a seat on the Upswell Mystery Tour. (this slow rally of sunsets from west to east.)

Some of the poems were first published in *Shearsman* (UK); *foam:e; the voice you speak with may not be your own;* and *Arryn Snowball Selected Works* (monograph). Thank you to the various editors for their interest and support.

About Upswell

Upswell Publishing was established in
2021 by Terri-ann White as a not-for-profit
press. A perceived gap in the market for
distinctive literary works in fiction, poetry
and narrative non-fiction was the motivation.
In her years as a bookseller, writer and then
publisher, Terri-ann has maintained a watch
on literary books and the way they insinuate
themselves into a cultural space and are
then located within our literary and cultural
inheritance. She is interested in making books
to last: books with the potential to still be
noticed, and noted, after decades and thus
be ripe to influence new literary histories.

About this typeface

Book designer Becky Chilcott chose Foundry Origin not only as a strong, carefully considered, and dependable typeface, but also to honour her late friend and mentor, type designer Freda Sack, who oversaw the project. Designed by Freda's long-standing colleague, Stuart de Rozario, much like Upswell Publishing, Foundry Origin was created out of the desire to say something new.